Endo

"Marc Hall has written this excellent book to assist you in discovering how to handle money, how to give money, and how to plan for the future. *Pursuing Spiritual Wealth* is written in a practical way where you can take it step by step and move toward a life of giving and stewardship, regardless the size of your bank account."

—Dr. Steve Gaines, PhD, Senior Pastor, Bellevue Baptist Church (Cordova, TN) and Past President of Southern Baptist Convention

"Marc Hall's book, *Pursuing Spiritual Wealth* is outstanding for a couple of reasons. First, he has done something that few others have in relation to stewardship. Most stewardship writing is about mechanics and principles, all well and good. But Marc goes beyond just the principles by giving us Biblical inspiration and daily encouragement to live out stewardship in every facet of life. Second, knowing Marc as I do, I can tell you that he is a serious practitioner in his personal life of the things he writes about. In fact, this book is so Biblically sound that I plan to recommend it to our entire congregation. While I am at it, let me recommend it to you as well."

—Ray Jones, Senior Pastor, Ridgecrest Baptist Church (Dothan, AL)

"This book will take you through a journey of understanding God's standard for stewardship and living it out for the rest of your life. It is designed for every person who wishes to better understand the connection between their wealth and spirituality. The process is very well laid out and will provide you with daily opportunities to apply God's truth. A great resource you will go back to again and again."

—**Leo Sabo**, President,
Christian Stewardship Network

"I am incredibly grateful for *Pursuing Spiritual Wealth* by Marcus Hall. To some, God gives much. To others, He gives little. But to all, God requires stewardship. *Pursuing Spiritual Wealth* is Biblical, practical, and a fantastic resource for those desiring to learn about and develop a stewardship mindset. Pastors will also find *Pursuing Spiritual Wealth* to be a great tool for helping church members manage their time, talent, and treasure for God's glory."

—**Art Rainer**, Author of *The Money Challenge*

"As the stewardship minister and a lay servant who's preached on the topic of stewardship and money dozens and dozens of times across many churches, I am familiar with the concepts. However, Marc does a fantastic job of setting up a journey that is great to read on your own but would also work in small groups or as a framework for a church-wide stewardship series. It covers complex topics in a simple, but not in a simplistic way. Marc takes you on a walk through Understanding, Adapting, Living, Planning and Giving by God's standards. It's about way more than money. It's about becoming truly rich by understanding how our concepts align with God's instructions."

—**Scott Maderer**, Owner and Stewardship Coach
with Inspired Stewardship

"If you want a solid understanding of Biblical stewardship in quick bite-sized chunks, then definitely pick up this book!"

—**Bob Lotich**, Founder of *Seedtime.com*
and Author of *Managing Money God's Way:
A 31-Day Devotional*

PURSUING
SPIRITUAL
WEALTH

40 PRINCIPLES THAT MAKE
YOUR LIFE RICHER

MARCUS HALL
FOREWORD BY RON BLUE

FREILING
PUBLISHING

Published by Freiling Publishing, a division of Freiling Agency, LLC.
P.O. Box 1264, Warrenton, VA 20188

www.FreilingPublishing.com

ISBN: 978-1-956267-14-3

Printed in the United States of America

Contents

III Living Out God's Standards

IV Planning by God's Standards

Foreword

I've had the privilege of spending most of my professional life working with individuals and couples helping them plan and manage their finances in such a way as to maximize their financial stewardship. What I have found is that God's word speaks to every financial decision that anyone can make at any time under any set of circumstances. When I shared that thought with a leading pastor of a large church, his comment to me has shaped much of my thinking since. He said, "if that's true, Ron, why is the church not seen as the center of financial wisdom?" There can only be one answer to that question. God's people do not believe God's word, which is very clear. It says in II Timothy 3:16-17, "All Scripture is breathed out by God and profitable for teaching, reproof, for correction, and for training in righteousness. That the man of God may be complete, equipped for every good work." God's word speaks to every area of my life, but especially to the material possessions He has entrusted to me. More is said about money in the Bible than any other subject. Why? Because money is the greatest competitor to the love of Jesus. (Matthew 6:24)

What I know is that God's word works in all of our financial thinking and decision making and it has three characteristics. First, it is simple. Second, it is relevant to everyone. Third, it is easily repeatable. So what has to happen? We as believers in the Lord Jesus Christ and the word that He's given us must act in faith on what He has to say. Every financial decision that is made begins in the heart and is a reflection of what I really believe, want, and value. The best way to make this operative in my life is to spend time daily thinking and meditating on what God's word has to say.

Marc has given us a book that can challenge your thinking and consequently your heart if you spend time meditating on what God's word is revealing. It is written very personally and very practically. My hope is that millions would take these principles and wisdom presented and apply them on a daily basis to their financial lives. Marc takes God's word seriously and applies it in every area of his life to the best of his grace-given ability. It's a privilege to write the foreword to a book that is so promising and helpful.

—Ron Blue

Introduction

My desire in you reading this book is for you to pursue spiritual wealth, not the wealth of this world. That worldly wealth may still occur, but you'll be so much more prepared if you've fixed your eyes on Jesus to be your guide. The Holy Spirit will instruct you how to use the gifts you've been given by God. Instead of concentrating so much on your inward satisfaction, you'll turn outward to discover all these opportunities for you to serve as a vessel for God.

You may be thinking, "I'm not really in a fantastic financial position right now." You're not alone, but you're also not excused from participating in God's plans for your life either. Let this book guide you through Scripture and discover the absolute best financial advice you'll ever find. There are over 2,000 verses dealing with money, finances, and stewardship to help you make better decisions going forward.

You'll gain a deeper knowledge and wisdom of God's truth, a more complete walk of faith with your Savior, and the ability to know that God can use you in so many more ways than you ever thought possible.

That's the great thing about God. It doesn't matter what you think about yourself or how ugly your past is. It doesn't even matter if you don't have much. The Lord delighted in the widow who gave two measly coins—*everything she had*—when everybody else who had more was stingy. (Luke 21:1-4) The rich could give gifts worth a lot more in earthly value, but God understood the widow's gift was everything to her.

It's all about your heart. It's all about your focus. And it's all about persevering in your faith to continue to grow closer and closer to Christ Jesus.

In *Pursuing Spiritual Wealth*, you'll discover forty principles that make your life richer... not by keeping score with your bank account and belongings, but by the fruit you'll produce as a more devoted follower of the gospel's teachings.

Know, Believe, Do.

I learned this from Ron Blue and designed the layout of this book to follow his advice. You will never change your behavior if you don't first understand and agree with the information presented.

Learn what God is teaching you, and then align your mind with the Truth. Only then will you be able to live out, plan, and give according to His principles through your everyday decision making and actions.

The Holy Spirit anticipates guiding you and inviting you into more kingdom work. Be enriched by His increased presence in your life.

I encourage you to keep your Bible open as you read through the chapters. Take time to discover the context of the Scriptures included in this book and understand better what God is specifically teaching you.

It will all be worth it the day you meet your Creator, and His first words to you are, "Well done, good and faithful servant... Come and share your master's happiness!" (Matthew 25:23).

I

Understanding God's Standards

1

Your Wealth Belongs to God

*Yours, Lord, is the greatness and the power and the
glory and the majesty and the splendor, for everything in
Heaven and earth is yours. Yours, Lord, is the Kingdom;
you are exalted as head over all. Wealth and honor come
from you; you are the ruler of all things. In your hands
are strength and power to exalt and give strength to all.*
—1 Chronicles 29:11-12 (NIV)

I tend to have control issues in certain areas of my
life. I have a hard time giving up power or dele-
gating. I feel like I can get the job done exactly like
I want it done, in the time it needs to be completed,
and in a fashion that is pleasing to everyone. This is a
problem of mine. Have you ever said, "Oh, come on,
I'll just do it myself" as you huffed in frustration? I
can't be the only one.

Do I tend to believe that I have more power, more
knowledge, and more sense than I really do? Of course,
I do. That's human nature. It's also a form of disobedi-
ence and sin when I allow myself to become god of my
own life. I've got all the answers. I know how it needs
to be done. Just get out of my way, and let me show
you how to do it!

1 Chronicles 29:11-12 explains to us that God possesses all the power, all the glory, all the majesty, all the splendor; not me. *Everything* in Heaven and earth is His. He is Lord and ruler of His kingdom. Okay, then why is this world in such a mess? If He has all this power, why can't God just say, "Here's how it's gonna be?"

That's what will happen. One day Jesus will return, and His control will no longer be in doubt to anyone. But until that time, we've been allowed to make our own decisions. We can choose to believe Christ is King and live our lives to demonstrate that belief, or we can continue to make bone-headed decisions that must leave God shaking His head at our arrogance and pride.

My breadth of knowledge and experience exists from May of 1976 until today. Even if I learned everything perfectly during that time, that span covers merely a blip of the thousands of years since God first created the heavens and the earth. Why do I get so cocky sometimes in thinking I understand everything about how this world operates? God allows me the opportunity to make my own decisions about how I live my life. I have all the freedom in the world to believe who I want, follow who I want, and imitate anybody I darn well please. But as I often tell my three girls, your choices come with consequences, both good and bad.

I can choose to live my days loving God and loving others, searching for ways to give generously, and proclaim the good news about His Son, or I can keep to myself, finding ways to avoid others and disregarding the disciplines that God has instructed me to live by. Sounds like a pretty miserable experience.

Even if I do get by okay (by my standards) here in this life, focusing on myself and not allowing Him to be Lord of my life, these lifestyle choices guarantee me that this life will be the best I ever see. All the promises of a glorious reunion in Heaven will be traded for an eternity in hell. That's not the outcome you should be trying to achieve.

Maybe our God really does know what He's talking about. He did create the world. He created each and every one of us. And He created the final destination of eternity for us. Maybe we should pay attention when He asks us to live a certain way. He has our best interests at heart.

- And we know that God causes everything to work together for the good of those who love God and are called according to His purpose for them (Romans 8:28 NLT).
- O my people, trust in Him at all times. Pour out your heart to Him, for God is our refuge (Psalm 62:8 NLT).
- And we are confident that He hears us whenever we ask for anything that pleases Him (1 John 5:14 NLT).
- Trust in the Lord with all your heart; do not depend on your own understanding. Seek His

will in all you do, and He will show you which path to take (Proverbs 3:5-6 NLT).

- Commit everything you do to the Lord. Trust Him, and He will help you (Psalm 37:5 NLT).

Our God longs and desires for us to listen to Him. Likewise, I plead to my daughters, please listen to me, I know what I'm talking about. I've been there. I've already made that mistake. I don't want you to make the same one. Now God didn't already make the mistakes like you and me, but He absolutely knows the truth and the best avenue for each of us to take.

It's time we relinquish the control we love so much. Talk to God. Listen to Him. It might not all make sense. Actually, a lot of it might not make sense, but that doesn't matter. That's living your faith. He knows best, and we should trust Him to guide us in the ways that He sees fit.

—⟐—

Apply Today's Truth

- Have you truly positioned God into His rightful position as Lord over all your life? There's no way to fully comprehend His playbook if someone or something else is standing in the way.
- In what areas of your life do you need to confess that Jesus is not truly your Lord? Right now is the

time to repent (turn away) from those idols that stand between you and Jesus.

2

God's Roadmap for Your Riches

"For my thoughts are not your thoughts, neither are your ways my ways," declares the Lord. "As the heavens are higher than the earth, so are my ways higher than your ways and my thoughts than your thoughts.
—Isaiah 55:8-9 (NIV)

God's thoughts are different than ours, and much better. On the surface, we sometimes believe we're further along than we really are when it comes to following God's commands.

He tells me not to cheat on my wife. Well, I'm not doing that. But He replies, "Yeah, I consider it cheating when you think lustfully about another woman" (Matthew 5:28). Oh, really? Well...

He tells me not to murder. Fine, easy enough. I definitely have that one covered. Or do I? His reply, "Yeah, but if you've ever held anger against a brother or sister, you're subject to judgment" (Matthew 5:21-22). Wait, what?

Am I really going as deep with my Father's commands as I should be? Just like with those other situations, God is asking much more of us than we like to believe. It's not just the physical act that God cares about with His children. What we learn from Jesus' Sermon on the Mount is how important our internal thought life is. That's where all of our actions originate (Matthew 15:18-19). We won't act in an inappropriate way if our minds are focused on the Word of God and how He wants us to behave.

Just like we can't leave God out of our thought life when covering the Ten Commandments, we can't leave Him out of our finances either. If we do, we'll never know His intentions for His money. Yes, His money. Every dollar in my bank account is a dollar that He's entrusted to me to use in a way that He approves. He's the owner. I act as the manager of His store. That's stewardship.

The owner has the right to declare how His resources are used. I've wasted a lot of God's money, time, and spiritual gifts He's given to me over the years. I haven't always been a great steward, not even close at times.

But my desire is to keep getting better. Our goal is to actually imitate Jesus, but we can't ever measure up to that. That's impossible. It doesn't mean we should stop trying each and every day.

Remember though, this isn't an expedition that we take on all by ourselves. I don't just show up to my first mountain climbing class and say, "I'll take Everest!" I have to work my way up to the big hill, but I can't teach myself. I need someone who's been there, done that; someone who has knowledge of the area and the ability to guide me and make me strong so I can face the treacherous journey ahead.

"For the Spirit God gave us does not make us timid, but gives us power, love, and self-discipline" (2 Timothy 1:7 NIV).

"He gives strength to the weary and increases the power of the weak" (Isaiah 40:29 NIV).

If I'm going to walk the path God has laid out for me, how will I ever succeed if I don't ask Him to guide me along the way? This isn't a solo journey, and I'm not a co-pilot. He is the only pilot. My desire for you is to say, "God, here I am. Please help me to understand your word and your desire for my life more and more each day." Your goal should be to walk one step closer to Him every day, every week, every month, and every year.

That's called the process of sanctification, or spiritual maturity. It's one step after another. You don't earn your long, flowing cape on day one and all of a sudden become Super Christian. It's a process. It's a never-ending process until the day you take your last breath. We can't be who we've always been. We can't act like we've always acted. It's time now to grow up and put the childish things away (1 Corinthians 13:11).

Warning: It's not going to be easy. But I can promise you, the more you dig into God's Word, the closer you get to Him, and the more you'll want to dig deeper. This is the power source you've been seeking for years. This is the stuff that fills that void that you've tried filling with everything else imaginable. It's probably where you've wasted a lot of your own time, money, and thought life over the years.

His thoughts are higher than my thoughts and His ways are higher than my ways (Isaiah 55:8-9). When we finally admit that and open ourselves up for understanding, rebuke, and correction, we get to see God's incredible power at work. He gives us everything we need to know about getting out of debt, saving for our future, and planning how to give to His church and His people in need.

Jesus came so that we may live a spiritually abundant life (John 10:10). I wish I had learned earlier what that really meant. Living with contentment, giving generously, managing God's resources in the intended way; it all leads to what we're all searching for.

Pray today that God will open your heart and that you'll be receptive to concepts and ideas that may sound weird and run contrary to what you've always believed and done. That's okay. That's what time with our Savior is supposed to be—our loving Father taking time to help us understand, learn, and adapt to the principles and precepts that will allow us to live the abundant life for which we've been created.

—◆—

Apply Today's Truth

- Do you spend time regularly with God in Bible reading, in study, in prayer? If not, what's keeping you from doing so? It's highly improbable that God will reveal His truth to you if you're not communicating with Him.
- Start praying now that God will prepare your heart as you read this book to embrace His principles for how He wants you to embrace your responsibilities as a steward of His resources.

3

Building Faith through Stewardship

His master replied, "Well done, good and faithful
servant! You have been faithful with a few things;
I will put you in charge of many things.
Come and share your master's happiness.
—Matthew 25:23 (NIV)
(Excerpt from parable found in Matthew 25:14-30)

This is an important study that will set the stage for every other chapter in this book. Truly understanding the role of a steward and what stewardship actually involves is crucial to being able to maximize the difference that God can make in your life.

Let's define "stewardship." It's the conducting, supervising, or managing of something. We have significant decisions we must make in order to become a great caretaker.

But let's move towards a biblical definition. That's what we're interested in. My favorite one comes from Ron Blue: the use of God-given gifts and resources—such as time, talent, treasure, influence, and relationships—for the accomplishment of God-given goals and objectives.

Think about being hired by a business owner. The owner has a vision for the company. Our responsibility is to understand what our boss wants and then to form our work duties around that vision and the goals we're given. If we don't, we get fired. We don't get to choose what we do and how we do it when we're managing the store for someone else. They make the rules.

This reflects our relationship with God. God's generosity has provided us with every talent we possess, every dollar in our bank account, and every minute that we have available during our day. Since God is the owner of these resources, He gets to make the rules. And He's decided that we should reflect His values and His thoughts when handling all those things. How do we accomplish this? If you haven't already done so, read about the parable of the talents found in Matthew 25:14-30. See how all three servants treated what their master provided for them to manage.

Who are identified as the good stewards in this story? The ones who took initiative in an attempt to grow what they'd been given. The bad steward? The lazy one who buried his head and his talent in the sand.

I think it's vitally important that we realize that God makes it clear it doesn't matter how much you have. What you give is proportional to the size you've been given. The servant who had five talents produced five more. The servant with two produced two more.

The owner was equally satisfied with both. God doesn't expect you to give something that you don't have.

God allows us to participate in stewarding His possessions because He wants us to be close to Him, to understand Him, and to be able to participate in the blessing of obeying Him, giving to others, and accomplishing His purposes. God doesn't *need* me for any part of His plan. I bring nothing to this party. This is simply God saying, "I want you to understand just a little bit about how this feels."

Here's the thing. If I'm working with God and following His guidance with my money, I'm showing faith through my obedience. I'm showing Him this money is not as important as He is in my life. If I'm willing to give to my church and others to whom He's called me to give, I am fulfilling the purpose He designed for me.

If that's not your single goal in life, then you need to update your goal list immediately. God is looking to see how trustworthy we are and to show us just how big of a part He really wants us to play in His ministry. In Luke 12:48 (NLT), we learn of one of God's promises. "When someone has been given much, much will be required in return; and when someone has been entrusted with much, even more will be required."

Consider how God increases our responsibilities as He realizes we can be trusted with more. If we open our eyes, shift our focus, and ask God what we can do, He will reveal to us a myriad of opportunities to show our love for Him. What did the owner do with the one talent that he took from the lazy servant? He gave it to one of the others who was producing and taking risks for God.

Remember this—God is not asking you to give away everything to everybody. You might ask about the rich, young ruler. (His story is found in Mark 10:17-27). Jesus demanded that he sell everything and give it away because He knew money was the one thing holding that young man back from total surrender.

My point—be responsible and take care of the lives that God wants you to touch, but do not feel guilty because He asks someone else to do something a little bigger and flashier. That's okay. That's His prerogative.

He doesn't have to explain or give us a long, drawn-out list of reasons why. I'm not responsible for my friend's job duties as God's steward. He is. Always help if you can and if it's appropriate, but don't take the responsibility and force something God didn't intend. That will not work well in the end. Oftentimes, something like that is done for your own glory, not God's.

If we are faithful, God will take the opportunity to use us even more. What does that mean for us? A deeper love, satisfaction, joy, and peace with our Savior. This should be our focus and our goal when it comes to our money, our time, and our talents. This is the heart of true stewardship.

—∿∿∿—

Apply Today's Truth

- Are you truly allowing God to use the resources He's given you to bring glory to His kingdom? Take a long, hard look at your money, your skills, and your availability... and how you're applying each one for God's purposes. What does your checkbook and calendar reflect toward your stewardship responsibilities?
- Are you willing to obey God and trust His judgment even when you don't really understand why He's asking you to take a step in an uncomfortable direction?

4

Spending God's Money

The earth is the Lord's, and everything in it.
The world and all its people belong to Him.
—Psalm 24:1 (NLT)

One of the absolute central points of our Christian faith is the fact that God created the world, all the people past, present, and future, and all the stuff that comes along with the world. He sent His Son to purchase His people with His blood atonement. He created us and has decided to allow us to work with Him to further His kingdom.

The money we earn throughout our careers, the knowledge, and spiritual gifts that each believer possesses, and our time on this earth; these are all resources that God has allowed us to manage for a time so that we can give them back in service to Him and His kingdom. He is the owner. We are His stewards.

We didn't go down to the courthouse and have everything deeded over to us so that we can decide how to best use all of our stuff. Jesus has deemed us caretakers of His gifts and has assigned us a responsibility for each dollar, talent, and hour that we've received.

Simply learning, believing, and living this lesson alone can make a colossal difference in your relationship with Christ. When we finally decide to allow the Creator and Owner of all things to call the shots, our lives remarkably become more peaceful and more fulfilled. That's because we're actually following God's plan for our lives.

My teenage daughter and I were having lunch in one of our favorite local meat-and-three establishments one afternoon. You know the type—some great country cookin' and a place where macaroni and cheese is considered a vegetable.

In walked an elderly woman by herself, mask on during the Covid-19 pandemic, with a book and a magnifying glass so she could read the pages clearly. It was hard to read much expression from just her eyes. I don't know why I assumed this, but my guess was that she was widowed and spent a lot of time alone. That's what it looked like, and that's what the Lord was telling me, I believe. Doesn't really matter because His main message that day was, "Ask for her check, pay for her meal, and don't mention it to her."

Years ago, I would've missed the opportunity to experience a blessing for her and me. Not today. I'm trying to be better about moving to action more quickly when the Holy Spirit nudges me. It's not that ten bucks is a huge deal. The huge deal is that I was in tune with my Father who was instructing me on how He wanted me to spend His money. He gave it to me to tend so that I could become a blessing to someone else.

This is how wonderfully spectacular our Savior is! Do you think He needs me or you to fulfill His kingdom missions on earth? Not by a longshot. But because He loves us so much, He designed this whole plan to actually allow us to serve alongside Him. He creates the opportunities to serve, and we're prompted to join Him. We're allowed to do service, not forced to. When you understand that it's not all yours, you're well on your way to a true life of stewardship.

I don't know if that woman was wealthy or poor; I have my assumptions. It might've been that I was experiencing a prideful attitude that day, and the Lord was reminding me exactly who I was and who He is. I don't know. And I don't care. I obeyed His request of me and will probably never know any result from that encounter. That might actually be the case a lot with God. Let Him sort it out. It's best that we consider ourselves on a need-to-know basis. Every now and then, we'll get to experience the thankful reaction. What a blessing that is!

What I do know is that God will direct me if I'm listening. He'll also direct me when I'm not paying attention. I'll just miss out on yet another blessing in my life of pleasing my heavenly Father.

Small events like this one allow me to loosen my sometimes-tight grip on "my" money. He may be preparing me for when He makes a bigger ask of my generosity. Hopefully then I'll be able to respond with a hand stretched out to give, rather than with a hand tightly gripped with those dollars safely tucked inside for my own personal use down the road.

Here's the neat thing—if I don't consider it mine to begin with, it sure makes it a lot easier to give away when God moves me in that direction.

Where do you have trouble understanding the fact that God owns it all? This isn't just a money question. God provided you with certain gifts, a finite amount of time, and knowledge that He expects you to share for the benefit of His kingdom.

Think about the things that you do well that earn you compliments... singing, writing, party planning, the ability to manage children well. It can be absolutely anything.

Now think about that talent from an eternal perspective. God, you gave this to me. How can I use this gift in a way that pleases you?

―⁓―

Apply Today's Truth

- What changes are needed in your financial decision-making process if you really believe God owns it all?
- What modifications should be made to your calendar, your commitments, and your attitude based on this same truth?

5

Work As Service to God

*Whatever you do, work at it with all your heart, as
working for the Lord, not for human masters, since you
know that you will receive an inheritance from the Lord
as a reward. It is the Lord Christ you are serving.*
—*Colossians 3:23-24 (NIV)*

The morning alarm is ringing and you begin
crawling out from under your warm blanket. The
mad rush begins of trying to accomplish some combination of breakfast, exercise, devotion time, and whatever
else your morning routine includes. Most days, it just
doesn't feel worth the effort. Maybe you think, "Why
am I putting myself through this every morning?"

The answer is simple. God created us to work. It
was the *very first* thing He assigned humans to do after
He created us.

Genesis 2:15 (NIV) says, "The Lord God took the
man and put him in the Garden of Eden to work it
and take care of it."

If God puts something at the top of His priority
list, I'm pretty sure we should take note of it. But pay
attention here. This is a big point of confusion with a
lot of folks who believe that work came about as part

of the curse of sin placed on our earliest relatives. That is impossible. Sin had not yet entered the world. It wouldn't take long, but work clearly came first.

Therefore, we can interpret work as a gift from God. If He created something for us, then consider it good. The Bible also makes it clear that God expects us to work if we possess the ability to do so.

In 2 Thessalonians 3:10-12 (ESV), Paul makes sure that message is clear. "If anyone is not willing to work, let him not eat. For we hear that some among you walk in idleness, not busy at work, but busybodies. Now such persons we command and encourage in the Lord Jesus Christ to do their work quietly and to earn their own living."

We don't really need to read between the lines to figure out what Paul was trying to convey to the Christians of Thessalonica. If you're able-bodied, if you have the opportunity, God expects you to get to work.

But why is this so important? What is it about work that God needs us to take so seriously? Think about the skills and character traits you develop by producing an honest day of work. You're honing skills that God provided, working with others in a coop-erative way, and producing something good in the process. Your work should absolutely be viewed as a spiritual calling. The particular job doesn't matter, but the work you do does.

Your job site, your office—these are the places that your representation of Jesus really matters. What are you portraying to the world? Who are you portraying to the world? If someone spent a few hours with you today, would they be able to recognize something different about you? The quality of your job performance, the way you speak to and treat other people, your joyful attitude even while enduring a difficult work environment.

Don't you think these qualities would help you stand out enough for someone to ask, "What's up with you?" They've just invited you to share your testimony. You've shown them Jesus—now you can tell them about Him too. You don't have to be preachy. You can simply share the ultimate joy and peace that a relationship with the Creator of the universe makes in your everyday life. That is living out your faith through your work.

We see several places in Scripture where Paul encourages us to remember that God is always present with us. He instructs us to perform to the best of our abilities in every facet of life, to offer up everything we do to the glory of God (1 Corinthians 10:31).

Like so many other times, we have to forget about our outside circumstances if we're going to focus on the eternal perspective. I've had jobs and bosses I didn't care for. So have you. God still expects us to look past these uncontrollable circumstances and to perform well because that's His desire for us (Colossians 3:23-24). It pleases God when we continue to show respect to those employers who don't show us the same respect (1 Peter 2:18-19).

The same joyful, peaceful attitude that we portray on Sunday mornings needs to be the real joyful, peaceful attitude that we experience and exhibit Monday through Friday as well. Take care of your responsibilities, help people when you can, and be thankful for the opportunity to earn a paycheck and glorify God at the same time. But remember the other part of our work lives that God prioritized as well; the need to take a break. Just a few verses before He mentioned work for the first time in Genesis 2, God introduced the idea of resting on the Sabbath.

I'm sure you realize that God didn't need to take a day off, but I believe there's a reason He mentioned the need to rest before He ever gave Adam his first assignment. This is God stressing the importance of refreshing your mind, your body, and your soul. The Sabbath isn't a day just for lying around. It's a time to relieve your physical and mental exhaustion... a chance to refresh yourself with the reminder of why you're doing your work in the first place.

Billy Graham once wrote, "Our work was never meant to become the center of our lives. That place belongs to God ... Someone who brags about working seventy to eighty hours (or more) a week probably thinks he is the master of his job—but in reality, he has become its slave."[1]

—⁕—

Apply Today's Truth

- Is there a need for an attitude adjustment with how you face your time at work every day?
- How can you show your love for God even more today at work? What skills, relationships, and opportunities are God presenting to you to transform your career into being a bigger part of your Christian ministry?

6

Finding Financial Contentment

Do not steal. Do not lie Do not deceive one another.
—Leviticus 19:11 (NIV)

God hates cheating in the marketplace;
rigged scales are an outrage.
—Proverbs 20:23 (MSG)

B e honest. Have you, at one time or another, stretched the truth just a little bit when it comes to your finances?

The cashier gives you back an extra dollar. You have plenty of opportunity to return it after recognizing the error, but you decide it's your lucky day. They should just be more careful next time.

That's not really what that deduction on my taxes is for, but we can make it fit. I need another write-off.

My spouse doesn't *really* need to know just how much I spent on this. Let's make sure we keep that from coming to light.

Every one of these instances is an example of being dishonest with your money. We don't usually look at most of them as being a big deal, but they all are. God didn't leave too much room for interpretation with Leviticus 19:11.

"Do not steal. Do not lie. Do not deceive one another." Is anyone confused by these words? You shouldn't be.

But what's the big deal? These things don't hurt anybody. But they do!

They hurt you, and they hurt your relationship with the Lord.

God hates cheating. God hates the thought that we have to lie about something, especially when we don't consider something that big of a deal! When we do something that God hates—otherwise known as sin—we hurt our closeness with our Creator and our Father. That relationship is fractured until repentance takes place, and we're able to mend it through the grace of God.

What is it about money that makes us able to deceive others with such ease about small stuff? We bow to the pressures of our environment that beg us to strive for as much money as we can get our hands on. When we think we've outsmarted someone else and we gain a few bucks in the process, we count that as a victory. So often, we don't even care that we've acted against our Christian values while doing so.

If our goal is to draw closer and closer to Jesus, we have to follow the example set by Him and His Father. It all comes back to how pleased we are with the blessings that Jesus has already handed down to us.

It seriously revolves around your overall contentment in what Jesus has done for you.

If you can honestly be content with your life and with how Jesus is leading you, the temptation for crossing over that line will diminish. It may never go away, especially if Satan knows that's your weak point. If you are a threat to Satan, then Satan is a threat to you. Being truly content with your life in Christ will weaken the opportunity that the devil has to take you down.

Hebrews 13:5 (NIV) says to, "Keep your lives free from the love of money and be content with what you have, because God has said, 'Never will I leave you; never will I forsake you.'"

Take Him at His word. Let God lead you and how you think. If you do, He's always right there when you need Him. The desires to cheat don't go away. It's just that now you have the Creator of Earth and the King of Kings on your side to deflect the arrows of Satan when they're tossed your way. It all goes back to making sure you've equipped yourself with that armor of God (Ephesians 6:10-18) so you can face the spiritual battles that await you every single day.

Every. Single. Day. It's important to understand that this is not a one-and-done deal. A soldier in battle doesn't wear his protective gear only when he feels like it. He knows he must be ready for an attack at all times.

You will be tested. When you're trying to grow in Christ and apply new principles to your everyday decision making, God will supply opportunities to test your progress.

And guess what? You won't pass every test with an A+. Odds are you'll fall flat on your face and get hit with several F-minus grades along the way. But here's the wonderful thing about our wondrous Savior! He's a God of second... and twenty-second... and 222nd chances.

Admit your mistake to the Lord. Apologize, repent, and learn from it. Dust yourself off, and start growing again. My most successful times in life have oftentimes come immediately after some of my absolute worst decisions and performances. That's where God gets your attention; when you've been knocked down to your knees.

Quit the rationalizing. Quit trying to find excuses for why you did what you did. The great thing about being honest? You never have to remember what story to tell afterwards. Just give 'em the truth.

—*∾*—

Apply Today's Truth

- Take an honest look at your habits. Is there somewhere in your finances that you've been taking a shortcut that you know is wrong? How do you rectify that immediately?

- Do you truly understand the importance of knowing your enemy's tactics and preparing yourself daily with the Holy Spirit and the protective armor of God?

7

Leading with Your Gifts

Remember your leaders, who spoke
the word of God to you.
Consider the outcome of their way of life
and imitate their faith.
—Hebrews 13:7 (NIV)

Y ou may not know it. You may not realize it. You may not even want to admit it.

But you're a leader. Someone, somewhere actually listens to you and cares about what you have to say.

I found an interesting definition of leadership written by Kevin Kruse in a Forbes article a few years back. "Leadership is a process of social influence, which maximizes the efforts of others, towards the achievement of a goal."[2]

You can have influence even when you don't have authority or power. It may not even come with a title.

- Are you married?
- Do you have children?
- Do you have friends?
- Do others report to you at work?
- Do you simply have co-workers?

- Do you teach a class of adults or kids at church?
- Are you involved in any type of group whatsoever?

If you answered "yes" to any of the above questions, then, guess what? You qualify as someone who's eligible to assume a leadership role. A center of influence.

Something you say or do has the ability to affect how someone else thinks, acts, or speaks. That's the audience God put you on *this* earth at *this* time and in *this* exact location to impact. He created specific gifts and placed them inside you to give you the opportunity to apply them to His work.

A good leader takes an interest in serving others. You have an opportunity to serve as a spiritual leader to those around you. Jesus expects this from you.

Paul writes in Philippians 2:3-4 (ESV), "Do nothing out of selfish ambition or vain conceit. Rather, in humility value others above yourselves, not looking to your own interests but each of you to the interests of the others."

Christ Jesus displayed a perfect life of leadership. He taught us to love out of humility, giving even His own life for the sake of everyone else's. Ephesians 5:1 instructs us to imitate that very love of our Lord.

Consider the strong Christian mentors who affected your understanding of living out the Scripture in their everyday lives. Were they gracious with their time and knowledge? Did they give generously from their wallets even if they didn't have much compared to the world's standards? You may not have known exactly how they spent their money, but there was no doubt they gave freely and liberally to their church and to other Bible-teaching organizations.

Remember, as God's children we're not *better* than anyone else, but we should be *different* from everyone who doesn't have a relationship with Him. (Romans 12:2) We are set apart by the righteousness of God. We have direct contact to the Creator. We can't allow the temptations and the riches of this world to deter us from our eternal purpose.

So, what if you died with a few more dollars in your bank account? God doesn't give a rip about those commas on your monthly statement. What He does care about: are you showing His love to a dying world? Are you living out the example Jesus displayed for us? A life of humility, a life of service, a life of allowing others to see the positive influence the Savior has on your sinful soul. Those are the traits of a good leader.

"When the righteous thrive, the people rejoice; when the wicked rule, the people groan" Proverbs 29:2 (NIV).

Our friends and co-workers aren't looking for more worldly leaders. We all know how frustrating it is working with deceitful, self-centered people. It only maximizes our horrible experience when those people hold places of authority within our groups or organizations.

It's up to you to set the Christian example. It wouldn't surprise me if you were the only example of Jesus many of your family members, friends, and co-workers experienced during any given week.

Jesus doesn't need us to proclaim His word, but how awesome is it that He gives us the opportunity to do so!

Still think you can't make a positive impact on someone else's life? Think again.

But rest assured, even if you don't witness a dramatic difference in their life, it absolutely makes an impact with the Lord. He sees you, and He recognizes your effort to follow the Holy Spirit's guidance in your life. That's the credit you're ultimately seeking.

Apply Today's Truth

- Sometimes we can't become the leaders God wants us to be because we're harboring bad habits. Are there areas of sin in your life that need examining, correcting, and repenting of to position yourself as a more effective leader for Christ?
- Where is God showing you opportunities to lead others in your life that you've never recognized before? Make a list, if necessary, of the roles you play in other people's lives.

8

Peace through Financial Hardship

*I am not saying this because I am in need, for I have
learned to be content whatever the circumstances. I
know what it is to be in need, and I know what it is to
have plenty. I have learned the secret of being content
in any and every situation, whether well fed or hungry,
whether living in plenty or in want. I can do all this
through him who gives me strength.
—Philippians 4:11-13 (NIV)*

Let's set the scene for the man who wrote these
verses. Think about Paul's past as a Pharisee before
experiencing his conversion on the road to Damascus.
Life was good for him. He was successful and climbing
the ranks. He was making money and gaining power,
characteristics that served him well as an important
member of a materialistic bunch.

As he writes these verses though, he's sitting in
a jail cell, communicating with his churches from
prison. What a contrast! Paul had lived both sides of
the spectrum, and he found contentment sitting in the

dirt on the floor of a Roman prison. He actually lived parts of his life both in need and with plenty.

Success wasn't defined by his stuff and his status. Sitting in a prison should've felt like the epitome of failure for his life, but it wasn't. Look at why he was there. He was more content now than when he was rich and persecuting Christians. Now he's saving them and has nothing but the shirt on his back.

Paul tells us in 1 Timothy 6:8-9 that as long as we have food and something to wear, we should praise Jesus for those simple things. If we fall into the trap of temptation and desiring so much more, we start believing all kinds of things that the devil whispers to us. We start a death spiral into ruin and destruction.

I didn't have much as a young adult just starting out. The first few years of many careers are not usually that lucrative, but working in small market local television news is one of the worst from an income perspective. Over the years, God led me through a different career path. My income increased, and so did my lifestyle. Only in recent years have I started to really consider how much we're spending as a family and how much of the focus was targeted primarily on us and not for what God intended for those funds.

It's so freeing to truly consider all your stuff, all your talent, and all your life as belonging to God. Do that, and you'll start looking for ways to give more. You'll start thinking things like, "I don't really need that" or "Do we need to spend that much on a vacation?" It's not because of guilt. It's because you'll start desiring certain things less and less than you did while being duped by Satan's tricks.

Contentment is being joyful and satisfied with where God has you positioned right now. This doesn't mean you shouldn't try to succeed more and grow in your career or your business. It doesn't even mean that you're not allowed to desire to grow your income. But why are you desiring those things? Are you looking for more ways to have fun and spend just on yourself or are you thinking "If I make more, I can give more"?

Experiencing true contentment has everything to do with what you truly desire. If you follow your heart, that's a recipe for destruction. Your heart is deceitful and sick (Jeremiah 17:9). I see it happen to me when my focus slips from eternal matters and Scripture and, instead, focuses on my current circumstances.

I'll start worrying about the way I feel about how someone treated me or I get depressed because I didn't earn those extra few dollars I thought I deserved. When my focus turns inward, I realize how much I *don't* have instead of everything that I *do*. Why can't I make more money? Why can't I be more respected? Why can't I be chosen for that honor? I, I, me, me... look where all of my thoughts are centered!

Perspective is everything. Almost immediately when I return to my source of power and knowledge and strength, when I get back to preparing a lesson or studying a devotion, those thoughts move back from me to Him. Now I start focusing on His will, not mine... His way of doing things, not mine.

My attitude changes. My problems don't instantly go away. But now I'm concentrating on how thankful I am for the way God has worked and is working in my life. I'm not so concerned with how I "feel." Feelings get me into a heap of trouble. God's Word is truth whether I feel like it is or not. Very seldom is doing the right thing going to be what I feel like doing.

That's why faith is so important in believing God's Word when I don't even think I want to. The things He tells me to do, the life He wants me to live, and the decisions that get me there don't come easily. They go against my flesh nature. Only by going against my feelings and in agreement with His Holy Word will I be able to accomplish all He wants me to do.

Trust Him that He knows best. Praise Him and thank Him no matter what your finances look like. It's all His anyway. He can give and take away as He sees fit. Be in a position where you are able to live with true contentment either way.

—◦◦◦—

Apply Today's Truth

- Perspective is crucial. Are your thoughts centered only on what you desire most or are you truly seeking contentment in Christ? If much of what you had was taken away today, would you still be able to proclaim your love and praise for your Savior?

- This is the end of the first section of this book. Review your notes and your thoughts from the past few days. How have you gained a better understanding of God's standards of how He expects you to serve as a steward for Him?

II

*Adapting My Mind to
God's Standards*

9

The Bible As Your Financial Guidebook

But the wisdom that comes from heaven is first of all pure; then peace-loving, considerate, submissive, full of mercy and good fruit, impartial and sincere.
—James 3:17 (NIV)

If any of you lacks wisdom, you should ask God, who gives generously to all without finding fault, and it will be given to you.
—James 1:5 (NIV)

First things first... it's impossible to start aligning our thought life with Jesus until we understand how to think from a spiritual standpoint. Dr. George Barna and his research team at the Cultural Research Center (Arizona Christian University) recently conducted a study of Americans and their worldview.[3] They'd previously established these six beliefs as essential for having a biblical worldview:

- Jesus lived a sinless life.
- God is the all-knowing and all-powerful Creator of the universe.
- Salvation is a gift of God and cannot be earned.
- Satan is real.
- A Christian has the responsibility to share their faith.
- The Bible is accurate in all of its teachings.

Here's the sad thing. In their research (American Worldview Inventory 2020), Barna's group found only 6 percent of Americans hold a biblical worldview and believe all of the list above. Even worse, the number was 12 percent just a quarter century ago.[4]

How can you expect to live a godly life if you don't share the same platform and beliefs as God? If you're having trouble with any of the statements, I encourage you to follow the advice found in James 1:5 and ask God immediately to share His wisdom with you. These things aren't a secret. He wants you to understand and embrace them. It's worth seeking out information from respected pastors or Christian friends to help find clarity.

God reinforces to us throughout Scripture He alone is owner of all the heavens and the earth—all the land (Leviticus 25:23), all the silver and gold (Haggai 2:8), every animal, wild creature, and the entire world (Psalm 50:10-12). Let's make sure we don't leave any room for doubt. We cannot begin living the kind of life God wants us to live until we get our attitude and perspective aligned with His.

Stop believing the money in that bank account is really yours. Stop allowing yourself to claim that comfortable home as your property. We must start genuinely believing *and* living as stewards of God's creation—not just saying it and giving Sunday School answers. Daily life decisions must be based on the fact that God allows me to look after His gifts for a reason.

Start investigating through prayer. "God, what is my responsibility here? Why did you choose me to be different in a certain way than somebody else? Why does this skill come so easily for me? Why did you bless me with more income than I actually need for my lifestyle?"

It's because He has a special plan for each one of us, and He's not making it up as time passes. His plan is already signed, sealed, and being delivered.

When you realize God has specific instructions just for you and your life regarding your finances and belongings, you start discovering your full potential in Christ. It's a wonderful "aha" moment. You'll see exactly why you were created and His expectations for your life.

In 2 Kings 6:8-13, we see the prophet Elisha being told by God the words the king of Syria was speaking while alone in his bedroom. He was able to thwart evil plans the king was conspiring.

How was Elisha privy to this information? It's because he was tapped into the primary source of all knowledge, power, and strength. He spent time with his heavenly Father every day in conversation, in prayer, and in communication. Because he was close to God, Elisha was able to see things in ways others weren't able to see.

When we tap into the knowledge of Jesus, our Father starts sharing some awesome stuff with us. His Scripture comes alive, and we start seeing things in ways we didn't previously. Was the same message there before? Probably, but we were too wrapped up in our own business and feelings to register what Christ was trying to tell us all along.

Our vision becomes so much clearer when the Holy Spirit is alive inside us and guiding how we see the surrounding world. If you're truly looking to God and asking Him for opportunities to use your money, time, and spiritual gifts for His kingdom, you better clear your schedule because He's about to reveal some magnificent plans for you. And when I say magnificent, they may not be large in scale in the way you're thinking. What He will do is show you how to affect possibly one person at a time in so many different small ways.

These are gratifying opportunities, and you're able to see the results right away by a smile, a "thank you," or a chance to describe what Jesus means to you and how He's affected your life.

However, God may also start revealing larger ways to serve Him with projects that will take more time and preparation. How does He do this? He starts laying it on your heart. An idea you can't shake, this feeling you really should be doing something about a certain situation. That's the Holy Spirit calling you into action. That's what happened to me. It's the exact reason you're reading this book now.

If you're all wrapped up in yourself, you'll totally miss out on a chance to bless others. You'll also miss out on God blessing you. His promises in Deuteronomy 28 are powerful. He lists several blessings He has waiting for us if we simply obey Him. I'm ashamed of the number of times I've missed out in my lifetime on ways to use His resources for His kingdom.

Here's one of the many remarkable things about our God: He's ready to give you another chance! Don't miss out again because your priorities are out of whack.

We are not our own ultimate authority as contemporary teaching leads us to believe. We answer to the God in control and in authority over all the world. He is our source of all knowledge and wisdom.

Where do we start in our search for godly wisdom? "Respect and obey the Lord! That is the beginning of wisdom. To have understanding, you must know the Holy God" (Proverbs 9:10 CEV).

—◦◦◦—

Apply Today's Truth

- How can you affect your everyday decision making by fully adopting a biblical worldview?
- What steps do you need to make to align yourself with God's wisdom?

10

Making Faithful Investments

This, then, is how you ought to regard us: as servants of
Christ and as those entrusted with the mysteries God has
revealed. Now it is required that those who have been
given a trust must prove faithful.
—*1 Corinthians 4:1-2 (NIV)*

Fulfilling the responsibility God gives us as stewards is determined in how we view Him. We've just discussed how important it is that we are able to differentiate His kingdom from this world. He trusts us to take care of His people by utilizing the resources He allows us to oversee.

Here's the funny thing: God doesn't need any single one of us to accomplish any one of the things He desires. He's God. At any point, He can simply make anything happen that He wants.

This entire process of stewardship is a system designed to help us grow closer to Him. It's our Creator allowing us the opportunity to participate with Him in His ministry. Think about it for a minute. The Creator of the universe loves you and me so much that He wants us to understand—as best we can—what it's like to help people connect spiritually with the kingdom of God.

Now, don't get too big-headed. We're not God. We can't save anyone. But how wonderful is it our God wants *us* to experience the exhilaration He does when others learn about Him and trust Him for the first time!

He gives us the story of the shepherd risking everything to go find the one missing lamb out of a flock of one hundred (Parable of the Lost Sheep—Matthew 18:12-14). He's not satisfied until all of His children are safe and content in a love relationship with Him. He is the only one who truly knows what's best for us and how we should be living our lives.

The opportunity we have is to take the money, the time, the spiritual gifts... everything on loan from our Master, talk it over with Him, and put those resources to good use in proclaiming His name, His word, and His kingdom.

1 Corinthians 4:2 says it is required that those who have been given a trust must prove faithful. It's up to us—with the Lord's guidance through study and prayer—to make the spiritually influenced decisions necessary to use these gifts wisely.

This is a daily, sometimes moment-by-moment, struggle to put away our old selves (Ephesians 4:22) and consider how our Christ would handle the situations we encounter. By relying on His guidance and word, we are drawing ourselves closer to Him. He tells us if we do that, He will also draw closer to us (James 4:8).

Our faithfulness matters. That's why God provided us with Hebrews 11—known as the Hall of Fame of Faith. In this chapter, we find all the encouragement we need to reinforce this truth. Since God promised us a life of following Him would be difficult, He saw fit to also show us the reward for doing so.

Read Hebrews 11—examine the faith exhibited by Abraham, Moses, Noah, Isaac, and Jacob, among others. See how often throughout time leaders of our faith had to rise up, get moving, and simply trust God... when they had no idea what was waiting for them around the corner. God told Abraham to get up and move in Genesis 12.

Where to? Didn't matter to Abraham. He simply got up and began his journey. This was just one of many times this great man of faith proved himself to God.

Noah built a ridiculously huge boat in the middle of dry land for what looked like no apparent reason to everyone. But God told him to, and Noah trusted Him. Noah's family was rewarded for his faith.

Acting in faith is a must, a non-negotiable. Hebrews 11:6 (NIV) makes that clear. "And without faith it is impossible to please God, because anyone who comes to Him must believe that He exists and that He rewards those who earnestly seek Him." That verse is one of the reasons your foundation in Christ better be strong when the clouds start to gather, the sky darkens, and the thunder and lightning begin to crash. When the force of the oncoming flood approaches, it's too late to start your data research on who God really is. You must already truly believe God's will is your best course of action.

Ever been driving late at night on a dimly lit unfamiliar street in the middle of a horrible thunderstorm? Wipers swishing on high, those long thick raindrops just pelting your car while the wind pushes the sheets of water in seemingly every direction. I've doubted sometimes I was actually still driving on pavement. Was that a white line or yellow line? Was that a line at all? It's confusing. It's scary. I didn't know what to do.

The middle of the storm is not the time to be finding your footing in Christ. This is the time to take that gigantic step of faith while recalling all those promises you've read and studied and all those times God has proven Himself to you in the past. Faithfulness is stepping forward when you can't see the next step. You don't know what the end result is going to be, but you do know your Savior is right there next to you, guiding your every step, helping you place one foot in front of the other in the midst of total darkness.

Your faith is proven through your obedience to God. This is your way to show and grow the faith you have in the Lord Jesus. By doing so, you will see how God always keeps His promises. You will also see your confidence in God's Word grow stronger and stronger each day.

—⦿—

Apply Today's Truth

- Is God asking you to take an uncomfortable step in faith for Him?
- Think back to times in your life when God has shown Himself to be true to His word. These are spiritual markers on your journey that help increase your confidence in Christ for the next time you need encouragement to move to action.

11

Finding Eternal Satisfaction

*But seek first His kingdom and His righteousness, and
all these things will be given to you as well.*
—Matthew 6:33 (NIV)

We've all been distracted by the nice shiny object in our lives that caught our attention at some point. Man, when I save up enough, I'm going to splurge for that, and it's going to feel good when it's mine. Only problem? It doesn't feel good. It actually feels worse when you get it. Why? I just bought the one thing I thought would fulfill me. I've been thinking about it, checking every few days to make sure it's still available, looking forward to when I could make my purchase.

But there's still an emptiness. The wisdom of Solomon, in Ecclesiastes 5:10, informs us "whoever loves money never has enough; whoever loves wealth is never satisfied with their income. This too is meaningless."

It's not really the actual money people desire. The number on the bank statement or the pieces of paper with numbers on them don't do anything for us. It's the value we believe it holds.

It's the power, the prestige, the stuff we believe it buys or guarantees. Do we need money to survive in today's world? Yes, of course we do. But where's our focus centered? If I love wealth, I will never have enough. I will always strive for another dollar.

It's impossible to ever be satisfied. There's always something else to desire and buy. You could spend weeks on Amazon's website and never see the same item twice. I can never be content because I could always earn more, grow more, and produce more. This way of life is hollow and absolutely meaningless.

Check out these instructions in Hebrews 13:5 (NIV). "Keep your lives free from the love of money and be content with what you have, because God has said, 'Never will I leave you; never will I forsake you.'"

God wants us to know He is the one single constant in our lives. He is designed to be the epicenter of where we find satisfaction in our heart, our soul, and our everyday life.

It's hard sometimes to discern the intentions of someone's heart, but we can definitely observe their actions, the things they do, and make judgments based on the fruit they produce or not.

Is the wealthy family giving money away and blessing others so they can be seen and recognized or are they driven by the Word of God to do so? I don't know. We probably won't ever know.

But is it a weird thought to think someone who is poor by earthly standards has a problem with materialism? We don't usually think so. But look at the examples all around us. People stealing from their workplaces, selling drugs, risking incarceration… all just to grab a few dollars.

If my heart can't be happy with God and thank Him for where I am today, I'm not content with what God has to offer. I'll be longing for more, and I won't care how I get it. Again, it's all a heart problem.

"But seek first His kingdom and His righteousness, and all these things will be given to you as well."

We're commanded to seek God first, and then one verse later in Matthew 6:34, we find additional instruction. We're told not to worry about tomorrow. There's enough to concentrate on today. Every day has its troubles. Don't jump ahead of yourself and waste time stressing out about the unknown. It's unhealthy, and it's sinful.

We run our internal gas tank all the way down to empty, and get all burned out by our career, our activities, and everything else we can find to try filling the gap. We move Christ to second place behind our drive for the next big deal, the huge promotion, the next career move.

What we tend to forget is that if we allow God to be God of our lives, He will actually help us accomplish more than we ever could have by ourselves with all the big decisions that come our way. By seeking first His kingdom, we're allowing God to provide for us according to His will and for Him to receive the praise and gratefulness for everything He provides.

That doesn't mean we simply sit back and say, "Well, God will take care of those things." We are called to work and work diligently—to give our very best to our jobs, our employers, and our careers. This pleases God as well, as we previously discussed. It's just making sure our priorities are in line with what the Scripture tells us.

Concentrate on what you need to do for God's kingdom. What do you need to learn? What is God trying to teach you? Who can you help understand the word better? If your focus is on doing what God desires in your life, you'll discover satisfaction, and He'll bless you to the measure He deems appropriate. When He does, praise His name and thank Him for His awesome generosity. Then make sure you're already looking for ways to share those blessings with someone else.

One of our main functions as Christ followers is to be a pass-through, a middle man, for the blessings of God. If this is your true default position, you will always be pleased and content with your position in His ministry.

It doesn't mean you can't strive to do more, be more, and produce more. You just have to make certain you're doing those things inside of God's will and you're focused on how you can give more as He increases your responsibilities.

—〰〰〰—

Apply Today's Truth

- In what ways are you filling the place in your heart that belongs to Jesus? What adjustments do you need to make to move Him back to His rightful spot in your life?
- Do you have trouble finding satisfaction in your life? Pray that God will help you realize and appreciate all the blessings He's already provided.

12

Relying on the Holy Spirit in Our Weakness

And the Holy Spirit helps us in our weakness.
For example, we don't know what God wants us to pray
for. But the Holy Spirit prays for us with groanings that
cannot be expressed in words. And the Father
who knows all hearts knows what the Spirit is saying,
for the Spirit pleads for us believers in harmony
with God's own will.
And we know that God causes everything to work
together for the good of those who love God and are
called according to His purpose for them.
—Romans 8:26-28 (NLT)

Talking about your weaknesses makes for a strange conversation. It doesn't feel right. It causes hurt and embarrassment. That's how we've been trained by the world to think. We're pressured to constantly display our strength and power to everyone instead.

That line of thinking flies in the face of our Christian faith. The Bible states, "He [God] gives strength to the weary and increases the power of the weak" (Isaiah 40:29 NIV).

On our best day, our ability and strength cannot remotely compare to what the Lord offers. We're only able to discover the true power of God when we get out of the way and allow Him to work supernaturally.

It's hard to admit my personal weaknesses. I can't let someone else know what might hurt me. That makes me vulnerable and opens up the chance for someone to dominate me or ridicule me. The things we experience in our daily lives force us to close up ranks and keep those weaknesses hidden deep within ourselves. Otherwise, we're asking for trouble.

Just look around at the hurt our Christian brothers and sisters experience, that you might be experiencing right now. We're not designed to deal with these types of hurt and pain on our own. Where has that gotten us? Broken relationships, deeply rooted distress that causes mental breakdowns, and even taking our own lives because we can't deal with it anymore.

If we're not designed to form the correct response to these situations, then what's the answer? Romans 8:26 tells us, "The Holy Spirit helps us in our weakness. For example, we don't know what God wants us to pray for. But the Holy Spirit prays for us with groanings that cannot be expressed in words."

What in the world does this verse even mean? Think about the special friend who knows your thoughts, secrets, and weaknesses unknown to the outside world. Our Heavenly Father has provided the Holy Spirit as our Helper... someone to know us intimately and to guide us through the perils of our daily lives.

Have you ever experienced confusion and pain so deeply you didn't even know what to say? The surprising large out-of-pocket expense, the unexpected call from the hospital, the spouse or significant other that blindsides you with a goodbye walkaway conversation. In that moment, you had no idea what to think, the words to speak, or how to pray. But God did.

Since God knows your innermost thoughts, your fears, your pain, His Holy Spirit understands you as well. He's able to communicate with God on your behalf, to supply the words you can't muster, if you'll ask Him to intercede for you in accordance to *God's will*. (Romans 8:27—emphasis added)

That's the tricky part. Keeping God's will at the forefront.

God's will won't always (or barely ever) match what my flesh desires in these situations. When we experience the devastating times in our lives, it's a proven fact we are not thinking clearly.[5]

Bad news connects with our emotional brain quicker than our rational brain. This fires up the immediate fear and anxiety. It's that scary feeling that totally overtakes you in the moment.

By the time you're able to process the information logically, panic has already set in. If you start making important decisions in the moment based on your emotions, those decisions will come from a place of fear, not rational thought.

Without the right focus and perspective, financial hardships can quickly cause you to make some horrible decisions. This is the feeling that causes you to immediately consider selling all your retirement investments when the market starts falling at a rapid pace.

You lose all sense of your long-term focus on investing for your future needs. You simply want the hurt to go away right now. Compare the short-term and long-term focus to your Christian faith. When you look at things from a worldly perspective, you're only considering the temporary outlook. Your decision-making abilities improve drastically when you instead focus on the eternal things of God.

We must choose during these trials to allow God and His Spirit to guide us to our correct response. Romans 8:28 reminds us, "We know that God causes everything to work together for the good of those who love God and are called according to His purpose for them." Praise God for that promise!

Don't expect your non-believing friends and family to jump onboard or agree with what you're doing or how you're doing it. Why would someone who doesn't love Christ, know His Word, or allow Him into their lives understand the ways of Christ? Why are we so often influenced by loved ones who don't share our same eternal perspective?

We should not trust in our own strength. It will lead us astray each and every time we experience turmoil. Paul addressed this idea. "But He [the Lord] said to me, 'My grace is sufficient for you, for my power is made perfect in weakness.' That is why, for Christ's sake, I delight in weaknesses, in insults, in hardships, in persecutions, in difficulties. For when I am weak, then I am strong" (2 Corinthians 12:9-10 NIV).

Our security, our hope, our trust must be in our Heavenly Father. Claim this promise made to all believers. But remember God is not working to make us happy—that's the world's objective. He is guiding us to be holy in His word and to fulfill His purpose for our very existence.

———

Apply Today's Truth

- In what ways are you attempting to attack problems with your own strength? What do you need to do to trust Christ to fight those battles with you?
- Reflect on decisions you've made recently under stress. Did you allow your emotions to guide your thinking? How could the results have improved had you slowed down, taken a deep breath, and consulted the Lord before leaping into action?

13

Avoiding a False Sense of Security

For the waywardness of the simple will kill them, and the complacency of fools will destroy them.
—Proverbs 1:32 (NIV)

Possessing wisdom only creates the capacity to make right choices. It doesn't mean you always choose correctly. Look at Solomon. The wisest man of all time made some huge errors in judgment even though he knew better.

He was blessed with all the wisdom, wealth, and respect the world could offer. He had the opportunity to minister and teach kings and leaders from other nations and became a fantastic ambassador for his Heavenly Father.

But that wasn't enough. He married hundreds of women for political reasons, gave in to the sin of idolatry, and eventually turned away from God.

Do we complete a project for God, something we know He was urging us to accomplish, and then kick our feet up in the recliner? "Well, that should do for now. Look at the great job I did for God."

It's amazing how quickly we make the 180-degree turn from serving our Lord for the right reasons and with the right attitude into a self-satisfaction mode of feeling really good about ourselves. You listened to God, and He directed you toward a task that was right smack-dab in your wheelhouse. It fit your favorite ministry with the spiritual gift that comes so naturally to you. You were even able to achieve that spiritual high. You answered the call and came through for Christ.

You completed the mission and then just tuned out for a while. It was time to rest. You earned it. (Sarcasm intended.)

We read so often in books, blogs, and articles about how to depend on God during the horrible times in life. But what about when life tends to treat us a little better than usual?

Your income unexpectedly increases. A few breaks fall your way. You've paid off some smaller debts and improved your cash flow. You might even be saving more and are building up a larger balance in your emergency savings account or IRA. The pressure eases a bit, and your confidence level rises.

During the tough times, you find yourself alone, scared, and out of options. It can actually be pretty easy to call on Jesus for help when you realize there's nobody else in the pit with you.

But let that confidence start seeping in. Complacency and self-satisfaction are quick to follow, and they create a false sense of security. When things are good, we get comfortable and resist leaving our safety bubble. We start relying on the money we saved and the career that's providing those funds in the first place. We even modify the way we think about ourselves.

It's so easy to rest on our laurels when everything is rocking along without any complications. We forget in the good times just how much we genuinely need Christ guiding us at *all* times in every aspect of life. Moses warned the Israelites, in Deuteronomy 8:14, if their hearts became proud, they would forget the Lord their God.

Jesus proclaims in Luke 9:25 (NIV), "What good is it for a man to gain the whole world, and yet lose or forfeit his very self?" Our time on earth is not designed to satisfy our own pleasures. We're called to serve God and His kingdom… always.

Choose to love and obey every task God sends your way. Don't get comfortable and lazy. By the time you find yourself in a rut, you're probably already gaining steam downhill.

How do I counter this complacency in my spiritual life?

It's common to plan on stopping your career at a certain age for retirement. Remember there's no retirement period in serving Christ. We are "on the clock" from the minute we profess Jesus as Lord and Savior until the moment He meets us at the gates of Heaven.

When you complete one holy assignment, praise God for allowing you to serve alongside Him, and then see where He can use you again tomorrow.

I wholeheartedly believe God gives us times of rest in our lives, especially by observing the Sabbath. We're designed to pause so we can recharge and refocus our energies on Him. But if you see yourself reaching a level and plateauing, it may be time to talk to God and see if He has something else in store.

I stray from the Lord's path when I neglect my Savior's teachings and fall back on my natural, flesh-centered instincts. Cruise control is a fantastic device for long trips down the interstate. It is not wise to set my life on cruise control just to see where it leads. Following my desires usually sends me over a cliff. It's a self-destructive behavior that leads me further and further away from where my mindset needs to be.

We know the truth. We understand what life is like with Christ at the helm. It's purposeful. It's fulfilling. It's where we're designed to be. Don't fall away from your faith. "We do not want you to become lazy, but to imitate those who through faith and patience inherit what has been promised" (Hebrews 6:12 NIV).

Complacency has no place in our walk with the Lord. Stay on guard. Keep moving as He instructs you.

Apply Today's Truth

- Are you remaining on task for God or has complacency set in? How does your attitude need to change to correct that behavior?

- Do you feel like you're wandering in your relation-ship with Jesus? Take time to pray for the direction He wants you to go.

14

The Small Things Matter

Whoever can be trusted with very little can also be
trusted with much, and whoever is dishonest with very
little will also be dishonest with much. So, if you have
not been trustworthy in handling worldly wealth, who
will trust you with true riches?
—Luke 16:10-11 (NIV)

I have three daughters—a college freshman, a second grader, and a kindergartner. We've moved through different life cycles over these past years that involve my wife and I trusting them to handle new situations with a growing amount of age-appropriate responsibility.

I remember the first time we allowed my oldest daughter to stay at home by herself. That first excursion was a quick trip to the store we knew we could finish in probably less than twenty minutes. There weren't too many horrible, scary, and dangerous things she could've done in that short amount of time.

It all worked out that first time. She had barely moved from the same position she was in when we left.

So, our confidence in her decision making started developing. Now at eighteen, it's fantastic. She can even feed, supervise, and tuck in the younger daughters while Mommy and Daddy get some much-needed time alone for dinner occasionally. But we wouldn't have started this process by stating to a young teenager, "Hey, we'll be back in three to four hours. Good luck."

She had to earn our trust. We saw she didn't make dumb decisions while she was home alone. She didn't open the door to strange people. She didn't tear up the house or have friends over when she wasn't supposed to.

Do you know this is exactly the process of trust that God is working in our lives?

Our Scripture for this chapter proves to us we must always be on guard. The smallest decisions we make matter to the Lord. How we handle our perceived less important matters plays a huge role in our spiritual growth.

I'll bet you don't even realize how many decisions you make during the day. Trace back to just the start of this morning. How many seemingly insignificant choices have you already made today? Your breakfast choice, taking a shower, your clothes, type of toothpaste, the route to work, who you talked to, everything you've said. It really is an endless list.

What about the things we should deem a little more important? Are you a faithful person? Do you get tasks done like you should at home and at work? Can friends trust you to call or text them back if they reach out to you? Do friends and family take a promise from you seriously?

If not, you may be failing with the little things. Today's verse from Luke doesn't only relate to money. It can describe so many facets of our life if we choose not to take the Scripture seriously.

How often have you ever asked the question: What's the big deal about something I neglected or handled the wrong way and just knew it... but I didn't care? The Holy Spirit tugged on your heart, but you totally dismissed the message with the thought that it really doesn't matter.

Read that verse in Luke again. It matters more than we could ever imagine. The couple of extra dollars we could leave as a better tip for someone who really performed and gave great service... the lunch we could purchase for an unsuspecting stranger enjoying a meal in the same restaurant as us.

God is watching our every move and thinking, "Can I trust you with these resources I've already provided you? And if so, could you be responsible and handle more of this in a way I approve as well?"

How we handle the small situations is a prime indicator of how we'll manage the big ones. If we take short cuts and allow Satan to overtake our thought process, we don't stand a chance of succeeding when the stakes are even higher.

Where do your thoughts of carelessness, omission, and indifference come from? The devil himself. Satan doesn't need to turn you against Jesus. He just needs to make sure you don't care enough to strive for excellence—excellence in the way you love Christ, excellence in the way you serve Christ, excellence in the way you put others first before yourself.

God commands us to set our thoughts on the good things He provides. "Whatever is true, whatever is noble, whatever is right, whatever is pure, whatever is lovely, whatever is admirable—if anything is excellent or praiseworthy—think about such things" (Philippians 4:8 NIV).

I desire to please my Creator and to do things that make Him happy with me. It's encouraging to hear people around me proclaim, "Great job! Knew you could do it! Wonderful work!" But what I desire even more is to hear my Savior say, "Well done, good and faithful servant! You have been faithful with a few things; I will put you in charge of many things" (Matthew 25:23 NIV).

Let God help you grow. He wants nothing more than to give you more and more responsibility in His kingdom work. But you have to earn that trust with Him by taking the small steps everyday as He prepares you for those larger assignments.

—⌘—

Apply Today's Truth

- Don't let the small decisions trip you up as you walk with God. Concentrate on specific instances when you've allowed selfishness or laziness to move you away from an eternal task. How can you ensure you'll be ready for your next opportunity to serve?

- Your thought life is vital in serving Christ. What changes need to be made so you can focus on those things that are noble, right, pure, lovely and admirable?

15

Money Is Not Your Master

*Don't you know that when you offer yourselves
to someone as obedient slaves, you are slaves of the one
you obey—whether you are slaves to sin, which leads
to death, or to obedience, which leads to righteousness?
But thanks be to God that, though you used to be slaves
to sin, you have come to obey from your heart the pattern
of teaching that has now claimed your allegiance.
You have been set free from sin and have
become slaves to righteousness.
—Romans 6:16-18 (NIV)*

We get so caught up with what words mean to us in today's lexicon, we overlook what God is trying to tell us sometimes. There aren't many words that evoke emotions like the word "slave." In conversations today, the word very likely carries a negative connotation.

But look at Romans 6:16-18. Paul asks the question, "Don't you know that you are slaves of the one you obey?" Here he's stating we make a choice every day by who we listen to, who we follow, who we give our time and attention. We are acting as a slave to whatever entity attracts that part of us. We allow someone or something to rule over and dominate our time and thoughts.

Take a few minutes to turn to Proverbs 4:20-27 and simply soak in the message. Solomon warns of this very thing. Pay attention to God's words, remember them, guard your heart, give careful thought to your movements, and keep a straight path toward the Lord.

When we deviate, evil lurks just off the straight and narrow path. It's not hard to find at all.

Then Matthew 6:24 (NIV) hits us with this statement: "No one can serve two masters. Either you will hate the one and love the other, or you will be devoted to the one and despise the other. You cannot serve both God and money."

We cannot satisfy the world's cravings at the same time we're satisfying the will of God. They don't match, and they never will. The most dangerous place we can find ourselves (but I so often do) is standing with one foot on the eternal side trying to follow Jesus and one foot crossed over the line enjoying the temptations and cravings of the world around us.

What we're really doing is not accomplishing anything, except making sure we will never grow spiritually to the place God needs us to be. Following God is not the same thing as choosing items from a buffet line. "I'll agree and follow commandments three, six, and eight but two, seven, and ten don't suit me. Just my style."

A favorite praise song we sing in my church choir is *Until My Voice is Gone.*[6] The first lines state:

No other King commands our full attention.
No other name's above all other names.
No other throne rules over every nation.
No other God deserves our highest praise.

How am I giving Him my full attention by picking and choosing which of His commands I follow, or which of His eternal assignments I take seriously? Last I checked, Jesus didn't jump up on the cross to prove a point and then slide on down once everyone saw what He could maybe, possibly, and was likely willing to do for us.

He made the full commitment. He was "all in" on doing everything it took to bear and pardon the sins of each and every one of us. Every agonizing second he spent in physical and mental torture that day, every lash that struck Him violently across the back earlier in the week... Jesus wasn't portraying a life dedicated to His Father while stuck feasting on the pleasures of this world. He was a slave to His Father's wishes only.

Look back at the activities you've participated in during the past week and the past month. Did you spend your time and your money on things that glorify God or were you glorifying yourself?

The precarious thing about Satan is he's tricky. He's good at what he does. Oftentimes, I can rationalize away a decision I make as a lesser of two evils to make it okay in my mind. Isn't it amazing how I can commit a sinful, evil act and still portray it as good because I need to continue to publicly portray my

Christian persona? That's Satan talking, the master of lies and confusion.

What are your priorities? Do they conflict with God's ideas of how you should be living? Be open to the Lord searching your heart to test you and to know your thoughts (Psalm 139:23). But be careful what you ask for... because He anticipates His introspection will lead to changes in your life.

Invite God to perform a needed checkup, and He won't have any problem diagnosing the heart of your sin problem. Be ready to face things about yourself you might not like or want to admit.

This is needed information though. It's crucial to remember this is the first part of growing again in your faith. You have to identify the sin, call it what it is, and seek repentance. Only then can you break apart from your earthly master and start work on repairing your relationship with God.

—⁓—

Apply Today's Truth

- How have you split your allegiance in recent days? Can you identify times that you've broken from God's will to follow your own?
- Please know that no matter how long or how far you've followed the wrong master, Jesus is ready for you to call on Him right now to break you free from your sin.

16

Learning the Simple Things

Whoever loves discipline loves knowledge, but whoever hates correction is stupid. The way of fools seems right to them, but the wise listen to advice.
—Proverbs 12:1,15 (NIV)

When my daughter Abigail was a first grader, we discovered her inquisitive mind. We hit that stage of life where all the wires were popping in her little noggin' at the same time. She started connecting bits and pieces of information together in her mind, and it was awesome to hear her working on the process out loud.

"How does the remote turn the TV off when it's not hooked up to it?"

"How is thunder and lightning made?"

"How do we know the day changes when we can't see it in the sky?"

I'm not making any of these up. I didn't say I had all the answers. Some questions are definitely easier to find the correct response to than others. YouTube has proven quite useful.

I'm trying to encourage her. I've told her the only way to learn new stuff is by asking someone. She's apparently listening to my instruction.

When do we convince ourselves this piece of advice is no longer useful? Do we just get to a certain point in life when we decide, "That's it, I've learned everything I need to know"? God tells us we should never get to that point. The Bible actually uses the words "stupid" and "fools" in Proverbs 12 to describe people who get to that point.

I know kindergarten through college was essential for soaking in information and learning about the world around me. Those first few years out of school... wow, what a crazy, confusing time. You're no longer a student, but you don't really feel like an adult yet. You're just starting to discover you don't know half of what you thought you knew as a college senior.

Here's what I've learned. If you're doing it right, that same feeling actually multiplies over time. The smarter you get, the more you realize you're not that intelligent. This mindset is priceless. It keeps you humble and thirsting for more knowledge.

The way we view money changes over time. It's often because our situations change. Early in life, making a $10 decision seemed challenging. It didn't take long before you experienced $100 decisions, $1,000 decisions, and higher. As your financial circumstances grow in complexity, your angst in forming a rational decision can as well.

Here's the good news! The state of your finances may change, but God's principles for dealing with them never will. His laws are transcendent. They're good yesterday, today, and tomorrow. Doesn't matter when you live, where you live, or how much money you have.

God's advice doesn't adjust like the rules of the world do. Does it get much simpler than these five principles?[7]

- Spend less than you earn. (Proverbs 21:20)
- Avoid the use of debt. (Proverbs 22:7)
- Build liquidity. (Proverbs 6:6-8)
- Set long-term goals. (Philippians 3:14)
- Rejoice in generosity. (2 Corinthians 8-9)

The game plan is simple. The execution can cause the challenge.

Although God shares His truths with us in Scripture, most of the exact situations in my life are not covered specifically. It's my responsibility to take what God tells me and use spiritual discernment to apply it to my life.

You must connect the dots between His message and your problem. You can't be in tune with Jesus if you refuse to communicate with Him. Christ expects me to regularly open my eyes, my ears, and my heart to understand what He wants to share with me.

If you're not doing that right now, make that A-number-1 on your list today! There is no way to face the ugliness and sinful nature of this world without having God's protective battle armor in place. The shots come fast and furious. If you're not prepared, you will be knocked down and knocked out.

It's essential to our spiritual health to understand what the Bible says about the way we think and act. It's absolutely a prerequisite that the Holy Spirit stake His claim and plant His flag in you so you're able to discern what is right and what is wrong... what is holy and what is sinful.

But it's not just reading God's Word, it's seeing it lived out in others. God speaks to us through the Bible, the Holy Spirit, and through each other. That's why small study groups, corporate worship with biblical teaching, and mentoring relationships are all so important. Why would you miss out on being able to glean so much wisdom from those who have studied it, lived it, gotten it right and wrong, and can now share their experiences with you?

The Bible literally refers to those of us who refuse to search out biblical advice as "stupid fools".

This is a crucial topic. Chapters throughout Proverbs repeat this same message.

- Proverbs 1:7—A fool despises wisdom and instruction.
- Proverbs 14:9—A fool makes a mockery of sin.
- Proverbs 10:18—A fool hides hatred with lying and utters slander.

- Proverbs 19:1—A fool has a perverted mouth.
- Proverbs 28:26—A fool trusts in his own understanding.

You are a fool if you do not continuously seek godly wisdom. Don't let stubbornness and foolish pride stand in your way of developing a closer walk with your Savior. He is waiting on you to call on His name, ask Him what you need to know, and to position yourself squarely into His will for your life.

"If any of you lacks wisdom, let him ask God, who gives generously to all without reproach, and it will be given him" (James 1:5 ESV).

―――◊◊◊―――

Apply Today's Truth

- You must prepare your mind and thought life for the battles you'll face. Pick at least one of the ways that we discussed to learn more about the Word of God. Start attending a small group or worship with Biblical teaching or seek out a Christian friend or mentor to discuss your relationship with Christ and questions you may have.
- Don't stop with this book. Continue reading. Find a biblical topic that interests you and find a study book or commentary to help you better understand a certain person or chapter of the Bible.

III

Living Out God's Standards

17

Your Spending Lifestyle

*Do not love the world or anything in the world. If
anyone loves the world, love for the Father is not in
them. For everything in the world - the lust of the flesh,
the lust of the eyes, and the pride of life—
comes not from the Father but from the world.
The world and its desires pass away,
but whoever does the will of God lives forever.*
—1 John 2:15-17 (NIV)

At this point, you've evaluated your biblical world-view and how it affects the way you look at finances. You've taken the time to dig deeply into what you believe and why you believe it. If you discovered changes needed to be made, hopefully you've asked God to help you with your thought life, and not just the wrong actions that stem from wrong thinking.

It's time to apply these principles to your everyday decisions. Let's begin with spending. Lifestyle spending usually exhausts the majority of a family's income. It can easily account for over half of every dollar earned or received. This category includes all the essential expenses, led by food and utilities, and then everything else like hobbies and vacations.

You can search throughout the Bible and find Scripture relating to your attitude of how to spend your hard-earned dollars, but you will not find any verse that dictates to you exactly how much you should personally spend, save, and give each month.

The message from Proverbs 21:20 (NLT) is a simple one to grasp. "The wise have wealth and luxury, but fools spend whatever they get." Don't spend more than you earn. Our generation has proven this a difficult principle to live out. If this is a problem for you to achieve, you must check your motives. Are you living a life to please God or one to please yourself? You're forced to examine your level of contentment. Have you made the decision, like Paul in the jail cell, to be content with the position the Lord has placed you in today? If not, your spending will always be a problem and prohibit you from saving for your family and giving to God's kingdom in the way that He wishes you would.

We are totally immersed inside a culture that demands our devotion to all the finer things this life has to offer. Every paid advertisement on your phone, television, and computer screen is attempting to move you to the action of purchasing an item, a service, or an experience. If you don't, you'll be left behind by everyone else who's already doing it.

Spending is not the problem. It's a heart issue.

If we truly focus on accomplishing contentment, peace, and joy in our Savior's plan for us, our spending habits will fall in line. The things we currently desire will change. We spend because our pride dictates we act like everyone else. We're uncomfortable being left out. It's too hard to go without.

But when we toss our pride into the backseat and start chasing the things of Jesus, our landscape changes. Our definition of success is oddly different than it has been for years. "Collect the most stuff." "I need the newest model." It turns into, "That's not as important as I thought it was."

Take a closer look at the passage for this chapter and the warning included. "If anyone loves the world, love for the Father is not in them." If your values match the ways of this world to the extent it causes you to blow through your income on frivolous, temporary things instead of taking care of the family and responsibilities that God has placed under your management, it is past time for an honest assessment. It is past time for you to reconnect with your heavenly Father and immediately request help in exploring the healthy, alternative, liberating lifestyle that only He provides.

> "Don't store up treasures here on earth, where moths eat them and rust destroys them, and where thieves break in and steal. Store your treasures in heaven, where moths and rust cannot destroy, and thieves do not break in and steal. Wherever your treasure is, there the desires of your heart will also be" (Matthew 6:19-21 NLT).

Your point of view needs refreshing. Everything we chase here on earth is bound for destruction. It dies out, it ruins, it goes away. But treasures in heaven— those are valuable and eternal. Those treasures exhibit your love for Christ and all that He's planned for you.

Even though today's lesson is concentrated on spending, building up your heavenly treasures is a sign of a heart that exists to please God. When you obey God with your lifestyle, your attitude, and your devotion, you are signaling to this world your desire to live out His purpose for your life.

You are telling this world you will not cave to its pressure to waste God's resources. For example, you choose to continue driving your older car because it's paid for. It may not be the newest model, but it works, and now you're able to use those available dollars to save, pay down other debt, or give to a ministry.

Comparison is one of the worst enemies of contentment. When we notice everything everyone else is buying, it's so easy to start coveting. When we see elaborate family vacation pictures and videos on social media, it can start a downward spiral that leads to a needless and harmful shopping spree.

When this happens, our focus is squarely concentrated on our friends and neighbors. If your eyes are locked on Jesus, this situation shouldn't phase you. Compare your righteousness to Him, not them.

Committing to a biblical lifestyle is crucial because it sets you up for financial success. Stop trading short-term happiness for long-term results. The only way to reach your overall goals is to establish a positive cash flow upfront. When your living expenses go down, it creates flexibility and improves your ability to move quickly when God requests your participation in His work.

—⟋⟋⟍—

Apply Today's Truth

- What are you thinking when you make a larger or unusual purchase? Do you desire something because someone else has it? Will the purchase help you appear a certain way to someone else? Seek the Holy Spirit's guidance on your true level of contentment. It's not always wrong to make larger purchases. This is simply an exercise to make sure of your motives.

- If you find comparison is a detriment to your decision-making, what can you do to rectify that? God provides us a way out of every temptation we face. (1 Corinthians 10:13) Do you need to adjust the shows you watch or the amount and types of social media you digest? The answer is prayer. He will provide the solution.

18

Budget for the Unknown

But while they were on their way to buy the oil,
the bridegroom arrived. The virgins who were ready
went in with him to the wedding banquet.
And the door was shut.
Therefore, keep watch, because you do not know
the day or the hour.
—Matthew 25:10, 13 (NIV)
(Excerpt from parable found in Matthew 25:1-13)

The ten women written about in this parable help us to understand the lesson of planning ahead. The five wise virgins made preparations ahead of time and weren't caught off guard. They weren't stumbling in the darkness trying to find what they needed when it was time to act. They were ready to be with their groom.

I cannot implore enough to people I counsel how important this lesson is. What is the only certainty when it comes to the economy, our health, and our lives in general?

Uncertainty.

Knowing this, why are so many people caught off guard when something tragic happens? Just because we don't know exactly where and when something will happen doesn't mean we can't prepare for those situations.

Can I prepare for any financial emergency that I *might* have? Of course not. This would be putting my trust in myself and not in Jesus Christ. He promises to give me everything I need (Matthew 6:25).

"For the Spirit God gave us does not make us timid, but gives us power, love, and self-discipline" (2 Timothy 1:7 NIV). God's Spirit doesn't make cowards out of us though. We shouldn't act in fear. We should use the knowledge, common sense, and discernment that come with being a child of God to be ready for certain situations we can't necessarily plan for.

What happens if your car gives out today on the way home from work? How do you pay for another one?

What happens if you or your spouse doesn't make it home alive tonight?

What happens if you're injured, can't work, but you're still alive and receiving treatment?

Where do you get the funds to take care of an emergency situation? If you're fully prepared, it means you have a smart place to get money from no matter the surprising event that caused the situation. That may come from places like an emergency cash account, work benefits, or a personal insurance policy.

Being prepared can be a difficult thing to do. It forces us to look ahead to scenarios we don't want to face. But that's the only way to be ready. You have to discuss uncomfortable possibilities with your spouse and family.

For instance, I discovered during a financial planning conversation with a couple that because the husband had taken a pension based solely on his lifetime, his wife would be in a heap of trouble if he died unexpectedly in the next few years. She wouldn't be able to survive too long based on what they had saved because a large chunk of their income would disappear.

After testing the scenarios, we were able to determine an amount of term life insurance that could close that gap and not break the bank in the process. Now, she's covered if something tragic happens. Additionally, the husband has a newfound peace knowing he's pleasing God with his actions. To me, this is one of the strongest forms of stewardship. We're using God's resources wisely and looking out for our loved ones at the same time.

1 Timothy 5:8 (NIV) reads, "Anybody who does not provide for their relatives, and especially for their own household, has denied the faith and is worse than an unbeliever." In context, this verse is describing how we should take care of specifically widows.

Don't let your spouse or your kids be left on the wrong side of a slamming door because you didn't perform your duties as the leader of their family. God expects us to take care of those He's entrusted to us.

If you work as an independent contractor or small business owner, this may be more difficult to achieve since you don't have a large company offering you all these benefits at open enrollment every year by simply checking a box. It may take some work to get things in order. That's fine. Do it.

Why is all of this important? I'll use our family as an example. My wife and I decided together for her to stay home with our children during their school years after she expressed a desire to do so. If we don't prepare correctly and something bad happens to me, I run the risk of forcing her back to work while she misses out on time she really wanted to have with them.

Our kids would then miss out on time with their mother we deemed beneficial during their formative years. I certainly don't like paying so many premiums for different types of insurance, but doing so has created a sense of peace that we're making thoughtful decisions for our family's sake. If the unexpected and uncertain happens, we've got a game plan in place to catch our fall. It's our job to be prepared. It's God's job to protect us.

I strongly feel God expects us to take care of our families in every reasonable way possible. It may require making sacrifices, but that's what we're called to do when it comes to protecting our loved ones.

—⌇⌇⌇—

Apply Today's Truth

- Do you need to initiate or review plans you've made for your family? Oftentimes, our situations will change without us making the necessary adjustments.
- In what ways can you better prepare your family for the uncertainty of the future?

19

Debt's Dark Hole

*Now listen, you who say, "Today or tomorrow we
will go to this or that city, spend a year there, carry on
business and make money." Why, you do not even know
what will happen tomorrow. What is your life? You are
a mist that appears for a little while and then vanishes.
Instead, you ought to say, "If it is the Lord's will,
we will live and do this or that."*
—James 4:13-15 (NIV)

Note: Over the next three chapters, we'll concentrate
on debt and the burden that it places on us. I wanted
to take some time to break down the subject since it's
one of the leading causes of broken lives and relationships in America today. Today's passage will concentrate on debt's long-term effects. We'll then tackle
your mindset and the mental aspect and discuss how
to move out of debt's dark hole.

Have you ever bragged on a resume or in an interview about being self-sufficient or independent?
Those can be buzzwords for certain employers, but
they don't paint an accurate picture of someone trying
to live and plan life as a Christian. I am a goal setter. I

plan goals every year for my business. I want to achieve results that prove that my business is healthy and growing. I also set goals for other parts of my life—my growth as a Christian, as a dad and husband, and for education purposes.

But if I'm making these plans all by myself without consulting God about them, I am presuming upon the future. That's not the smartest route to a successful life. Am I allowing God to lead me down the path He wants me to travel or am I forcing my way down a back road He has no intention of me navigating? We start doing the same things when we amass debt in our personal lives. Everything may look great when I first purchase that house.

I know we were looking in a lower price range... but this house is fantastic! It's got everything we could ever want... even more rooms than we need, a pool, a huge yard for the kids to play. I know it's a little more than we planned to spend, but it's perfect. Is it though? By stretching the parameters of that house application and mortgage payment for the next thirty years, I'm assuming that my financial situation will at least stay the same, if not get better over time. But what if it doesn't?

What if your company has to downsize and you find yourself sitting on the outside looking in? All of a sudden, that perfectly do-able loan payment is now an uphill struggle to make every month. In addition to your career struggles, now you're adding financial trouble to that nightmare scenario. Not a great combination.

When our stress levels go up, it is proven that our decision-making abilities decrease quickly. We move into a dangerous zone of concentrating on trying to find the short-term answers. Just do something to make it better *right now.* That's when the downside trajectory toward impending disaster gains steam quickly. We totally shatter any notion of fulfilling our long-term goals until we can make the hurt go away.

What if we had made a decision not to stretch the amount of debt that we signed up for, just because the banker told us we could? By presuming on your future, you are adding a risk factor to your long-term plans that you can easily avoid. Why did we need to buy so much house? What made it so hard to stay inside our price range? Pride, ego, selfishness. Probably seeing our friends down the street and the new house they just purchased.

Every dollar you presume inside a large loan or amount of loans is a dollar you leverage against your financial health. Every month when you shift those extra funds toward a gigantic loan payment, you lose the ability to ever do anything else with that dollar. Are there examples of times when a loan makes sense? Of course there are, but not nearly as often as you might expect or already have in place now. That's what's gotten so many Americans in trouble over the past few years. It's hard keeping up every time a friend takes a luxurious vacation or spends wildly on a new water toy or fancy vehicle.

What is God asking you to do? What is He giving you permission to do when you're making financial decisions? If you're not including Him on these conversations, you're missing out on the wisest advice you'll ever find on the topic. The Holy Spirit is quick to let you know when you're stepping out of bounds. If you don't feel good about a decision, or you know your spouse is not onboard with you, it's time to bring that train to a screeching halt. Don't do it. Abort the mission. Retreat quickly.

On the other hand, nothing beats the ultimate peace you receive when you hit the bullseye in the center of God's target for His will for your life.

Allow God the opportunity to change things up. He'll throw you a curve ball you aren't ready for. It's that phone call that brings the bad news that changes everything about how you pay bills each month or how long you or your spouse will actually be around. Verse 16 in James 4 follows up this chapter's Scripture with the statement, "As it is, you boast and brag. All such boasting is evil." Know that your plans can (and oftentimes will) change dramatically at some point. Make sure to leave God room to work in your life.

Apply Today's Truth

- Did God play a part in your last decision to take on a new debt? How did you feel during that process? Were you guided by Him or did you ignore His advice?
- If your current income took a dramatic decrease tomorrow, would that cause you a great deal of financial stress in paying your creditors? If so, it's time to rethink how you're currently managing your debt.

20

Releasing Debt's Control

The rich rule over the poor,
and the borrower is slave to the lender.
—Proverbs 22:7 (NIV)

I t's payday. You've just looked online to confirm that the funds have hit your checking account. Now it's time to divvy out this week's paycheck. Your tithe is the first to come out. We'll discuss more on this later, but this is number one! Now you start doling out everything that has to be paid.

Your employer's already taken out taxes. Gotta pay those or they throw you in jail.

Next up are loans—credit cards, car loans, mortgages, personal notes. Wow. Are you uncomfortable with how much of your earnings are being used to pay for your possessions?

Just look at how much Americans suffer from taking on an excess of debt. According to a Bankrate online article (March 2020), Generation X households (born in the 1960s and 70s) now carry an average of almost $136,000 in loan obligations.[8] Many age groups are even increasing debt over the past few years.[9]

How does debt take control of your life? Twenty percent of people say they spend half to *all* of their monthly income toward debt repayment.

If you don't make these payments on time, what happens? Someone comes and gets your stuff or throws you out of your home. That kind of pressure can build up loads of mental exhaustion when things start getting tight.

Every dollar you're spending on that current loan or credit card is another dollar that can't be used for anything else in your life—giving, saving, or investing for the future. You will forever decrease your potential lifestyle, net worth, and flexibility by continuing to pay debt year after year after year.

"Well, I'm getting by now. I'm okay."

I understand, but as we just discussed, we must prepare for uncertainty in this fallen world. Before the spring of 2020, did anybody expect to have their hours cut back dramatically for a few months or lose their job completely because folks around the world were getting sick from a virus? The added pressure just became a noose tightening around your already stressful situation. How much more enjoyable and satisfying would it be to have choices like: Could I build up my emergency savings? Could I give more away? Could I save more for my retirement?

This is the life Jesus wants for us. He desires for us to make decisions concerning our lifestyle that will allow us to live the abundant life He spoke about in John 10:10 (ESV). "The thief comes only to steal and kill and destroy. I came that they may have life and have it abundantly."

When we live a life full of burdensome debt, we relinquish all the options we have of fulfilling the reasons God shared His resources with us in the first place. You are now a slave to your debt and not to your Creator.

The debt turns up the heat on the pressure cooker. Don't believe me? Owe more on a loan than you have sitting in your bank account for a few days. All of sudden, anxiety increases. Your worry multiplies. What's wrong with that? Worrying is a sin that dominates you and every thought you think. Multiple Scriptures instruct us not to be afraid. In Matthew 6:25-34, we're told not to worry about our life. Then what do I do? What is the answer? How do I deal with the mess I find myself in?

"Come to me, all you who are weary and burdened, and I will give you rest. Take my yoke upon you and learn from me, for I am gentle and humble in heart, and you will find rest for your souls. For my yoke is easy and my burden is light" (Matthew 11:28-30 NIV). Jesus is reassuring us here. First, He hears us. Second, He understands. And third, He wants to help.

If you find yourself in the position of being enslaved to your debt, and you're serious about turning things around, let God help. It won't be easy, and it won't happen overnight. All of your spending decisions year after year got you here. Don't expect to make everything right immediately.

The first thing you must do is put down the shovel. Quit digging deeper and making the hole larger. It's time for a lifestyle change for all decisions moving forward. Dig into God's Word. He will absolutely be clear about the way He wants you to be doing things. Now you won't find the verse that says, "You don't need to spend $100 on that expensive dinner," but you will experience the mind of Christ explaining how you should think and how you should act. It's not necessarily the spending that's killing you; it's the mindset you have that allows you to make those decisions so easily.

Here's one of those terrific aspects of God's character. When I finally give in to His way of thinking and start tuning in to what He wants for me, my whole decision-making process starts to change dramatically. The things that were important before are no longer important anymore. What we thought was freedom before—buying more things and enjoying more of the good life—is now seen for what it really is. It's a way for Satan to confuse you, to waste your opportunity to put those dollars toward the work of the kingdom.

"No temptation has overtaken you except what is common to mankind. And God is faithful; He will not let you be tempted beyond what you can bear. But when you are tempted, He will also provide a way out so that you can endure it" (1 Corinthians 10:13 NIV).

Apply Today's Truth

- Are you drowning in bills and debt? How did you find yourself in this situation? What is it about the way you view money that needs to change?
- Ask God for guidance, wisdom, and a place to rest. He will help you if you're willing to evaluate your decision-making process and learn how to be content with what you have.

21

Lifting the Burden of Debt

*Trust in the Lord with all your heart and lean not on
your own understanding; in all your ways submit to
Him, and He will make your paths straight.*
—*Proverbs 3:5-6 (NIV)*

So much of God's Holy Word spends time
explaining the freedom that Jesus achieved for us.
He lived His human life, died a horrible death, and
arose from the grave to conquer sin and the devil.

If it was such a big deal that God provided us
freedom from our sins, why do we choose to remain in
bondage when it comes to our finances? We've established allowing your obligations to pile up takes a toll
spiritually, mentally, and even physically.

So how do you find your way out of a horrible debt
situation? You must decide you know it's the right
thing to do. The Bible tells us as much. We learned
that in our last chapter.

Do we actually believe Scripture enough to make
it a priority in our lives? The Bible does not state that
having debt is a sin, but it sure doesn't encourage the
lifestyle either.

"Let no debt remain outstanding, except the continuing debt to love one another, for whoever loves others has fulfilled the law" (Romans 13:8 NIV).

"Do not be one who shakes hands in pledge or puts up security for debts; if you lack the means to pay, your very bed will be snatched from under you" (Proverbs 22:26-27).

This verse describes the freedom we experience when we shed the need for owing someone a debt. Nothing can be taken from you because of the inability to make a payment or debt every month. I've told folks many times it's amazing how little amount of money it takes to live when you don't owe anybody anything. Experiencing this truth in life greatly decreases the pressure you carry that causes harm in so many ways.

Many people don't even realize the actual extent of this burden. I was surprised the day my wife and I paid off a huge debt a few years ago. As I was handing the final check to the bank cashier, I felt a tear form in the corner of my eye as I made the final payment. I didn't expect that to happen. I hadn't fully understood just how big of a weight the debt placed on us.

When God takes control of your thoughts, you're able to start devising a wise plan for moving yourself out of debt. Figure out what you're actually trying to accomplish and then set a goal. The goal must be written down, measurable, attainable, and include an endpoint. All of these steps are crucial. Otherwise, it's just a good idea and will never be implemented.

Then track your progress over weeks, months, and years. Sometimes you'll get ahead of the goal, and sometimes you'll fall behind. Don't get discouraged. Even if it takes longer than you thought it would, you're still making progress. The key is to readjust your goal and keep trucking ahead.

For instance, you want to pay off your car loan as quickly as possible without straining your finances. You decide you can afford to pay an extra $200 of your income toward the outstanding balance for the next fifteen months. Doing this allows you to pay an extra $3,000 of principal payments during that time period. Your reward? A quicker reduction of the balance and several months shed off the life of the loan.

You state the goal. You measure your progress. You possess the ability and the drive to achieve the goal. And you know the finish line.

Here are the results from your hard work. For the first time in a long time, you start to see, feel, and taste actual progress being made on your dreaded financial situation. You're able to catch your breath and see there might actually be a light starting to shine up ahead.

Christian financial teacher Ron Blue has commented that he's never met someone who was unhappy about paying off their house. This stuff weighs on us. Why wouldn't it? It's something God wants you to do away with so you can remove the albatross and free up more resources to use for His kingdom.

He will help you achieve this goal if you set forth the effort by using your intelligence, thought process, and desire to truly follow His instruction as part of your stewardship responsibilities.

I love seeing and hearing the excitement from friends who conquer their mission to pay off debt! All of a sudden, other goals that were not possible just a short time ago are now back in the mix due to an increase in monthly cash flow. One-by-one you start knocking off the credit cards and car payments. The momentum starts rolling.

It's exciting when the conversation can turn to other ways to use your resources. You can begin giving more or bulking up your retirement accounts. These results are not beyond your reach anymore.

The decision to pay off debt is one that follows God's plan for stewardship in your life. You're managing the resources He provides in a way that you can now better take care of your family and His kingdom.

You'll start distancing yourself from the chains of debt—all the worry, concern, and anxiety. Now you can experience true freedom with Christ at the helm and allow Him to lead you toward true biblical prosperity and spiritual wealth.

—◦◦◦—

Apply Today's Truth

- It's time to take action. Organize your overall debts and monthly expenses associated with them. Start prioritizing which accounts to attack first. You can do this by size, time remaining on the loans, or a combination of factors.
- Pray for God to guide you through this process. Set measurable and attainable goals for how to start your debt reduction. Start making progress today.

22

Don't Throw It Away

When they had all had enough to eat,
He said to the disciples, "Gather the pieces that
are left over. Let nothing be wasted."
—John 6:12 (NIV)

J esus had just fed over 5,000 people without breaking a sweat. He believed and spoke the meal into existence. Why was He so concerned with making sure the leftovers were picked up? What's His message to us here?

He hadn't worked hard. He hadn't spent a lot of money. But He immediately instructed the disciples to start collecting the leftovers. Do you think they wondered internally, "What's the big deal? Do we really need all this food?"

I believe there's absolutely no coincidence that each disciple was able to fill up and hold one of the twelve baskets on his own. Each one of them had the opportunity to carry a basket while probably wondering how in the world there was enough food for everyone in that crowd to have a meal and *then* have enough remaining to collect and use again. Jesus made sure the miracle was personal to each and every one of His core group of students. God takes whatever we offer Him, and He multiplies it beyond anything we could ever imagine.

But what else does it say that Jesus gave these instructions immediately after the crowd had barely swallowed their last bites? Verses 11 and 12 show Jesus praying for the food and passing it out to everyone. Twice we see it noted that every member of that crowd had all they needed to become full and satisfied. You know somebody went back for seconds and probably thirds. Everybody had all they wanted. The next words recorded were of Jesus sending the disciples back out to the crowd to collect the leftovers.

How upset do my wife and I get when our small kids refuse to eat a large part of their dinner that ends up going down the garbage disposal? Especially if it was a meal Christy spent a lot of time and effort on? When this happens, it upsets me for her love, care, and time spent preparing the meal to literally be thrown down the drain.

I was taught the value and gratitude of finishing everything on my plate, both out of thanks to the hands that physically prepared the meal and to God who provided the resources for the meal in the first place. It's hard to understand that lesson as a young child when you've never wondered where your next portion of food was coming from. It's not just our kids. How much food, money, fill-in-the-blank do we waste every day in our land of plenty and excess?

Jesus wants to make sure we don't forget the lesson of wastefulness.

As you've already detected, many of the verses we've discussed so far can actually be applied to our lives in numerous ways. We all benefit from wasting less of our monetary capital. Consider the other resources supposedly under our watchful care that we allow to slip away as well.

God allows us only a limited amount of time on this earth. It may seem longer depending on what you're doing and what line you're standing in. But seventy to eighty years in the grand scheme of things is a minuscule amount of time. What do we find ourselves doing while we're here? Several studies have figured Americans spend over 40 percent of their lives looking at screens of some kind.[10] Over thirty years of our human existence is filled staring at computers, televisions, and phones.

What else could we be doing with all our time? Paul answers the question in Ephesians 2:10 (ESV). "For we are His workmanship, created in Christ Jesus for good works, which God prepared beforehand, that we should walk in them." We are designed to resemble Jesus, and I do not recall our Savior taking too much vacation time during His thirty-three-year earthly ministry. He rested as we all should, but He didn't let a day get away from Him without affecting His Father's kingdom in a positive way.

How often have you turned off the television or finally put down your phone late at night and realized you hadn't spent any time with Jesus that day? I'm not terribly proud of my answer to that question. A large part of our stewardship duties involves simply showing up and participating, not wasting another of the gifts from our sweet, generous God. He created us for good works, not to save ourselves, but to glorify Him in all that we do. If the Holy Spirit is alive in you, you should thirst to spend your time searching for ways to know Jesus better, to serve His people, and to draw others to Him.

Think eternally. Get out of the temporary mindset. We use all kinds of excuses—busyness, avoiding our problems, and just simply being lazy. Don't let this world confuse you to the point of being wasteful with your time and talents.

"Take no part in the unfruitful works of darkness, but instead expose them" (Ephesians 5:11 ESV).

"Let us lay aside every weight, and sin which clings so closely, and let us run with endurance the race that is set before us, looking to Jesus ... who for the joy that was set before Him endured the cross, despising the shame, and is seated at the right hand of the throne of God" (Hebrews 12:1-2 ESV). Our Savior lived with eternal purpose. He commands us to do the same.

—◦◦◦—

Apply Today's Truth

- Do you spend too much time staring at a device every day? Set some ground rules, and give yourself an allotted amount of time each day to use your device. At the same time, arrange a scheduled appointment with Jesus and His Word if you need to begin a regular time with Him.
- What other ways are you being wasteful with God's gifts? Talk to Him and discover how to better serve Him with your time, talents, and money.

23

Money and Marriage

That is why a man leaves his father and mother and is united to his wife, and they become one flesh.
—Genesis 2:24 (NIV)

We've established that without hesitation the absolute best source for all financial decision making comes straight from the Bible. But what happens when the Bible doesn't exactly spell out the situation you're currently facing? We understand the general guidelines that God wants us to know, and we're following them.

But these fall somewhere between the cracks. You could go either way without sinning. How do we make that decision?

If you're married, the answer is simple. Talk it out with your spouse. God established the marital relationship for companionship, yes, but also for you to have someone who knows you inside and out. Someone who was placed on this earth to spend their days with you. Someone to share the ups and downs of life. And yes, someone to have a different vantage point than you sometimes.

Scripture tells us in Mark 10:6-9, "At the beginning of creation God made them male and female. For this reason, a man will leave his father and mother and be united to his wife, and the two will become one flesh. So they are no longer two, but one flesh. Therefore what God has joined together, let no one separate" (NIV).

Our world has distorted this Scripture in all kinds of ways. God knew exactly what He was doing when He said "male and female". Like always, He had a plan in place. His expectation was for men and women to be created as equals, but with differences.

These differences are vital when it comes to making important family decisions. Remember, any financial decision you make involves and affects your spouse just as much as you. You are now operating (or should be according to God's definition of marriage) as a single unit.

Focus on the Family published an article in 2015 entitled "His, Hers or Ours?" that perfectly illustrates this truth. In it, the author Chuck Bentley compares our marriage relationships to our two hands.[11]

Have you ever tried performing mundane daily tasks with one hand tied behind your back? Getting groceries out of the car, picking up your child, driving? It all seems much harder. Your two hands were actually designed to work together.

Now consider husband and wife like right and left hands. Either hand may be stronger at performing certain tasks, but when they act in concert with one another, production increases. The results are magnified compared to what one hand can do by itself.

I've seen the story several times over the years involving the cooperation of horses. One horse can pull 8,000 pounds by itself but when teamed with another the production doesn't double, it actually triples to 24,000 pounds. They complement each other, work together, and are actually much stronger than simply two horses working individually.

God's goals for your marriage include working together to bring about a greater result than you going it alone. One of you may have a stronger knowledge or spiritual conviction in an area of finances that can lead the team to make better and stronger money decisions. Don't discount the role your spouse can play even if they don't always show interest in the financial stuff.

Here's a scenario I see play out often. One spouse does everything on the financial side... balances the books, makes all the decisions, and keeps everything to themselves. While I agree there should be someone who takes the lead and accomplishes the administrative tasks for the family, the other spouse must always know what's going on and how to run the operation themselves.

Doing this builds trust and a sense of teamwork that will only make these important and sometimes very difficult conversations even easier to have.

In my family, I handle the everyday stuff like paying bills and saving for the retirement accounts. But I pay close attention when Christy and I discuss something, and she reveals a strong idea that may be different than mine. I find there's usually a reason. God speaks to us through Scripture, our pastors, and Christian teachers, but I absolutely believe He also uses our spouses in the same way.

Look at the sound advice found in Ecclesiastes 4:9-10 (NIV). "Two are better than one, because they have a good return for their labor; if either of them falls down, one can help the other up." God created your marriage to act as a partnership. You each have your assigned roles, but you're meant to work as a cohesive unit.

I don't care who has the most knowledge of financial things. The decisions you make affect both of you, your children, and your financial future. God has connected your two lives for many reasons. You must strive for unity in financial decisions based on His Word and His values.

———⟳———

Apply Today's Truth

- Do you or your spouse make all the financial decisions and keep all the important information to yourself? Plan a family discussion to make sure the other spouse understands how money flows, how bills are paid, and how decisions are made.

- Money can be a challenging topic to discuss as a couple. Don't be afraid to pray together to ask God how to formulate discussion time and to build a plan that helps both of you stay involved in the process.

24

Budgeting

*Suppose one of you wants to build a tower. Will he
not first sit down and estimate the cost to see if he has
enough money to complete it?*
—*Luke 14:28 (NIV)*

Let's be completely honest. Very few of us love
building a family budget and working hard to
stick to it. It's tedious. It's revealing. It's difficult.

But it's also biblical.

As we discuss so many different principles of stewarding the gifts of God in our everyday life, developing and living by a budget frequently provides the remedy needed for our financial problems.

How often have you looked at your checking account register or online banking and wondered, "Where did it all go? We should've had enough to take care of everything this month."

It's because you're allowing your money to slip away unnoticed. There's no rhyme or reason involved in your decision making. You make spur-of-the-moment decisions for unneeded or larger-than-needed items.

Look at the verse at the start of this chapter. Who would ever begin a large project of building a home or office building without taking some time to figure out what the costs might be? You can't ever expect to complete a task precisely to the penny of the projected price, but it's a lot easier to adjust if you know what to expect.

How in the world can you adequately save for emergencies, pay off your debt, and grow a proper retirement account while funding your everyday needs if you have no plan in place? It's not going to happen magically.

It's your job to direct your money where it should go. In Proverbs 27:23-24 (NIV), we find excellent advice on the matter. "Be sure you know the condition of your flocks, give careful attention to your herds; for riches do not endure forever, and a crown is not secure for all generations."

The writer is urging us to act responsibly and with foresight. We're not given an option. If we're acting as faithful stewards, part of our responsibilities include looking and planning ahead. An online bank survey in 2019 showed that 1 in 5 Americans spend more time planning their vacations than managing their money. Another 34% said they spent an equal amount of time on both. The total accounts for over half the people surveyed.[12]

Let that sink in. As a culture, we are more engaged in focusing on a few days at the beach or theme park than we are in the direction and purpose of the plans

God has for us over our lifetime. One should not compare to the other.

When you budget, you're able to prioritize how your money is rationed. Remember, money is a tool God uses in our lives. He's promised to provide us with more responsibility if we can be trusted with what we've been given in the first place. (Luke 12:42-44) What better way to show our diligence and make the best use of what we already have?

By practicing this principle, you and your spouse determine how much you tithe, how much you save, how much is used for debt, and how much you spend for other things. You're keeping a record of what you plan and then notating what actually happens. These two numbers will never match at the end of the month or year, but I'll bet you're a lot closer to your desired results than you were before. Worst case scenario, at least you can quickly determine what needs fixing if things go wrong.

It's a discipline. It's not supposed to be easy. You don't honor God with your perfection. You honor Him by working hard to live life according to His instruction. You honor Him by discovering His will for your life and positioning yourself directly in that path.

Think about the limited things you can actually do with God's money. You can spend it, give it, pay for your debt and taxes, and save it. All of your decisions fit into those few categories. The Ron Blue Institute uses a pie graph to record the categories *Live, Give, Owe,*

Grow.[13] Figure out the percentages you've designated to these four areas, and your eyes will open widely to opportunities where you can serve God more.

How high is your spending rate? How low is your giving? Do the results fit the stewardship mindset you're trying to achieve? If not, start budgeting where you can figure these things out in real-time, not just months down the road.

This isn't meant to be a lesson of step one, step two, and so forth. It's just an application to the principle you want to master. The main theme I'm stressing is to understand why it's important to budget and know where your dollars go.

To honor God, we must focus on the way He wants us to do things. By being purposeful with your income, you're quickly aware of any problems of over-spending or neglect in your finances.

Adopting a more concentrated effort helps you to grow dependence on your Father. For a lot of you, using a budget may be a new concept. If you're trusting God and doing something He's asking of you, *especially* if you don't fully understand why, you're growing in your obedience. This moves you closer to God. This should be a goal in everything you do.

—◦◦◦—

Apply Today's Truth

- Be completely honest about your spending habits. Are you living above your means right now? Review every dollar you spend in cash, by credit card, bill pay, etc., for a three-month period. You may be shocked at the results.
- Now you're able to perform an effective personal analysis. Start pointing out places you're spending that could be decreased or cut out immediately. Think heavily of the distinction between needs and wants. The more tightly squeezed your situation is, the more difficult it may be to determine needed changes. Take your list of expenses to God. The Holy Spirit will be happy to guide you to form a healthier plan.

IV

Planning by God's Standards

25

God and Goal Setting

Unless the Lord builds the house, the builders labor in vain. Unless the Lord watches over the city, the guards stand watch in vain.
—Matthew 7:24-27 (NIV)

Are you a checklist person? You better believe I am. I require an exhaustive list either physically or mentally of everything I'll need before starting a project. What are the expectations? When does it need to be done? How much time will it take me? Do I understand all the details involved? The inside of my cranium can be an exhausting place.

Even when I arrange answers to all those questions, there's still one task I must complete before moving forward. Unfortunately, it's one I frequently neglect.

Don't start any project, any plan, any major event in life without seeking the Lord's guidance first. He may not always give you the entire blueprint, but He will absolutely provide the go-ahead needed to get started on the right path.

Not understanding the finished result is oftentimes a tremendously difficult thing we experience. My brain informs the rest of me that it needs to see a model of how this all turns out before I take action. God is happy to remind me knowing the ending shouldn't be my first concern. I hear Him whisper, "I will guide you where I see fit, and I expect you to come along with Me."

God's been leading me down a path of growth for the last couple of years. He told me I needed to complete a certain educational course before I was able to move forward in specific areas of His work that interested me. I asked, "Well, what's next?" His response was to trust Him and allow Him to be God. I'm on a need-to-know basis—a condition mentally excruciating for someone with my mindset.

But isn't that exactly what faith is? Something I can't see. I have no idea how the next chapter in my life is going to turn out. However, if I'm in tune with my Savior, He will guide and direct me along the way.

My pastor wisely told me to be in a season of just saying "Yes" to God (probably good advice most of the time anyway), but to do so without spending too much energy on what lies ahead. He added to enjoy the current environment I'm in while I'm developing. Be content! (Notice a theme?) It's during this time that I experience exceptional growth, knowledge, skills, network, and all kinds of other resources to prepare me for God's next chapters.

In John 15:7 (NKJV), consider another of our Father's loving promises to us: "If you abide in Me and My words abide in you, you will ask what you desire, and it shall be done for you."

The genie verse, right? We don't rub a lamp and let God know our three wishes. Far from it. "If I abide in Him"—if I give control of my thought life over to God, guess what happens? I start thinking like Him. The things He deems important will start becoming important to me.

Now when I ask Him for something, I've got a much better shot at asking for something He wants for my life anyway. He just needs me to desire the same things He has planned.

My selfish, me-first wishes transform into unselfish, what-would-God-want-for-me wishes. It's true. It's actually tremendously liberating and exciting. When you start living your life looking through your God-lenses, you see opportunity after opportunity start to open up in front of you. "Where did that come from? I didn't know I could help my friend in that way," or, "I never thought about that specific giving opportunity."

If I set goals quickly without thought and without prayer, I'm simply throwing my wishes down onto paper and stating what I'd like to have happen over time. Nothing inherently wrong with that—I just can't expect those things to be spiritually blessed by God (even the "Christian" stuff) if I haven't talked to Him about it and received His go-ahead.

I'm absolutely guilty of this. I set goals every year for my business, my family, my education, and my health. Some years, I'm simply trying to get something on paper and wrap up the activity. "Just add

15 percent growth." "Yeah, what I did last year sounds about right. Just copy that for next year."

When setting goals, you must remain open to the opportunity for God to take you somewhere you've never been before. The kicker? Allow Him to drive and not show you the roadmap. That's a tough proposition.

Most of us feel the need to understand exactly how point A moves to point B and how point B transitions to point C. Jesus seldom operates that way. If you see everything perfectly laid out step-by-step, you're not exhibiting faith. You're simply doing your own thing in your own way.

> "And without faith it is impossible to please God, because anyone who comes to Him must believe He exists and that He rewards those who earnestly seek Him" (Hebrews 11:6 NIV).

Seek God's will for your life and then make His goals your goals. This pleases Him, and it allows Him to reveal to you His reasons for creating you in the first place.

Apply Today's Truth

- What big decision is currently looming in your life? Have you spoken to God about it? If not, do so now.

- Do you have trouble trusting God to take a step in faith when you can't see where the next step leads? Pray that He will supply you with the courage needed to build your faith to the point of complete obedience.

26

Plan, But Don't Worry

And my God will meet all your needs according to the riches of His glory in Christ Jesus.
—Philippians 4:19 (NIV)

We all have things we look forward to later in life during our retirement years and after the kids have graduated and started their own lives. I've heard all kinds of dreams and motivations from people over the years.

"I can't wait to spend more time with my grandkids."

"I want to be able to work if I *want* to, not because I *have* to."

"We really just want to make sure we have enough money to last us the rest of our lives for the things we need."

These are all admirable goals to set, to aim for, and then to achieve. But goals take planning. Planning is not just okay with God, it's encouraged by Him. In Proverbs 6, ants are described as small yet wise creatures. They prove their smarts by collecting and storing their food during the summer so they'll have ample nutrition during the cold winter months.

He wants us to think ahead and plan to take care of ourselves and our families. These activities are part of our responsibilities of stewarding a family—taking care of them by using our available tools and resources.

1 Timothy 5:8 (NIV) reads, "Anyone who does not provide for their relatives, and especially for their own household, has denied the faith and is worse than an unbeliever."

Be careful though. There's a fine line between planning and worrying. When we plan, we should take time to talk with God about what He's envisioning for our future. As a result, we can align our thoughts with His thoughts and make sure the goals we're setting are part of His design for our lives.

Jesus' parable in Matthew 6:25-34 perfectly illustrates how our thought process should function. He literally states in verse 25, "Do not worry." He proceeds to explain how intentionally He provides for the birds of the air and the lilies of the field. If He shows so much affection for these birds and flowers, how much more will He care and provide for you who His Father designed in His own image? Your blueprint originated as a model of your heavenly Father.

"Therefore do not worry about tomorrow, for tomorrow will worry about itself. Each day has enough trouble of its own" (Matthew 6:34 NIV). The time we spend planning for our future is time well spent. We take it a step too far when our planning crosses the line into experiencing anxiety and fear of what tomorrow may bring.

We're oftentimes confused about where the line dividing planning and worrying is located. When you're properly following God's lead and setting goals for saving, paying off debt, and retirement income, God actually alleviates your worry and concern. I've witnessed the transformation in husbands and wives after engaging in proper goal setting and then enacting their game plan. If you continue to be consumed by apprehension about future what-ifs, you're actually experiencing interference in your relationship with Christ.

By seeking His wisdom, we're simply tapping into the exact reason God designed us. Think about purchasing a large children's Christmas gift... one of those that requires assembling from scratch. You get home, spread out all the pieces, parts, and unidentifiable objects all over the floor. Where do you start? The best place to look is the instruction manual... written by the company who created, designed, and manufactured the product.

When I'm planning for my life and my family's future, how should I start the process? Spread all the pieces of information and important data out on the table, and ask the one who designed it all. God, where should I start? How should I handle this situation? What are you telling me is the most important goal I should have during my young adult years? In the years leading up to retirement? What about my years during retirement?

By taking this approach, you're including God in everything from the beginning, just like the Bible instructs. Why is following this method so important? What usually happens when you're fighting so hard for something God doesn't have planned for your life? It doesn't even have to be a sin or necessarily a bad thing.

You may desire a new position at your company. You just know this is the perfect next-step for your career. But it's not God's plan. Is the situation going to work out if you're fighting your Creator every step of the way? How did it work out when you battled your earthly parents on something they didn't want you to do?

It's a beautiful peace to experience when you're walking hand-in-hand with the Savior. When you know you're exactly where He wants you to be right now, this minute. But don't think for a second that we're now scot-free. On the contrary. We will still fight the daily battles and the long wars as part of our earthly existence. It's still a world wrecked by sin.

But now, you're moving along exactly as the Lord instructs. You are living out your faith. You're trusting Him to guide you step-by-step when you can't see the finish line and have no idea what's waiting for you around the next corner. You've found the sweet spot. The unexplainable peace. To know that even when this world kicks you from behind and knocks you off your feet, you are positioned directly in the center of God's will. You know He's guiding and teaching you through all of life's daily battles with Satan.

When I'm running the race on my own, the worry creeps in quickly. It happens when I'm relying on my own power, my own knowledge, and my own experience. What a recipe for disaster. Now I'm forced to come up with the right answer. I've got to be prepared when the unexpected crossroads appear.

My pastor once told our congregation God has never come to a fork in the road. He knows all the routes because He created the routes. I just stand in confusion wondering what to do next. At best, I've got a 50-50 shot of making the right choice. Why would I settle on a plan where I might please God but the odds are just as good I'll make the devil's day as well?

You don't have to settle. Your 100 percent correct heavenly solution is waiting on you to seek and follow His instructions for your life. Seek first *His* kingdom and *His* righteousness, not yours. Doing this will help you alleviate the worries and fears that consume you when you're making all of life's challenging decisions on your own.

Apply Today's Truth

- Is there a part of your life that causes extreme fear and anxiety? Why is this the case? Have you sought God for His advice concerning your situation?
- It is a good thing to plan. Have you begun thinking about how to save, pay off debt, and

prepare for your future? These are parts of fulfilling your responsibilities as a good steward of God's resources. Seek a Christian mentor or professional advisor for guidance on how to start the process.

27

Displaying Patience

Blessed is the one who does not walk in step with the wicked or stand in the way that sinners take or sit in the company of mockers, but whose delight is in the law of the Lord, and who meditates on His law day and night. That person is like a tree planted by streams of water, which yields its fruit in season and whose leaf does not wither - whatever they do prospers.
—Psalm 1:1-3 (NIV)

These verses are labeled "The Way to Happiness" in *The Financial Stewardship Bible*.[14] Compare the attitude of the believers mentioned in this Scripture with the attitude you encounter when studying the Word of God.

The Law of the Lord makes them full and satisfied. They're able to concentrate on the law amidst the distractions circling around them. They think about it and meditate on it day and night. They study, they focus, and they soak in the knowledge of God day after day after day. But they don't always experience the desired results in their own time. Their fruit is produced only when it's time and in season.

The lesson of patience is not a fun one to learn. D.L. Moody once wrote, "So few grow, because so few study."[15] How do you expect to be prepared and filled with God's Word if you're not willing to put in the time it requires? You can't grow biblically without focusing on the Bible.

We expect results for everything right away. I can't believe I'm sharing the fact I'm old enough to remember not having a remote control to change channels on the home television. As a child, I was my own remote control. Can you imagine the nuisance today of having to take the time to actually stand up, take a few steps to change channels, and then repeat the process every time you wanted to scan the stations? It's exhausting to even think about.

How frustrating is it when we can't see the fruits of our labor right away? We're experiencing a great deal of this agony with our younger daughters right now. I've coached my girls in softball. Those first t-ball seasons are centered around simply learning the fundamentals.

The girls want to be independent and do things themselves. I want them to as well. But learning and grasping new things takes time. It's hard to start at a major league level when you're not even consistent with putting your glove on the correct hand. They're learning new skills like hitting the ball properly and fielding a batted ball the correct way without getting badly injured. The girls get frustrated when things don't turn out well. We expect the best results when we haven't put in the proper time yet to master the skill.

Don't be fooled if you experience some good early results. God uses the contrast between grass growing and trees growing in Psalm 92:7 (NIV). The psalmist writes, "The wicked spring up like grass and all evildoers flourish, they will be destroyed forever."

The wicked sprout up like grass. In my neck of the woods, when we receive consistent rain during the summer, the mixture of warm sunshine and moisture creates a fertile environment for small plants to grow quickly.

These plants may be plentiful, but they don't have staying power. It doesn't take much force from a late afternoon thunderstorm to knock over and knock out some smaller versions of vegetation. But the force must be much stronger to knock down a mature tree that's taken years to spread out its branches underground and grow into a mighty structure in the backyard.

The small plants grow rapidly for now but are not sustainable over the long term. The tree is slow to mature, but when it does it not only produces its fruit, but it can also withstand forces that other smaller plants cannot.

It's absolutely frustrating to see others producing fruit while we're stuck in a growth stage. Or worse yet, when we're stuck in a stage where we don't feel any movement at all. Why can't I be doing what they're doing? Remember, stewardship requires a focus and concern with God's plan for us, not someone else.

Quit worrying about what somebody else thinks or how you appear to them. If you're focused on God's growth plan for yourself, you are positioned in the right spot. You have no idea what He's preparing you for. It may take an additional battle, experience, or relationship to get you where God needs you to flourish.

Patience is a dirty word to most of us. I cannot stand waiting. I am terribly impatient. I'm the guy who scopes out the lines at the grocery store and will make multiple moves to different lines if I believe it will help me check out sooner. There, I admit it.

God isn't concerned with our timetable. He uses His own schedule for tracking our growth and our production. His plan is designed so we'll connect with other believers when it's time to make a maximum impact together for the kingdom.

Galatians 6:9 (CEV) encourages us to hang in there when things don't go according to our plans. "Don't get tired of helping others. You will be rewarded when the time is right, if you don't give up." It's not a sprint, it's a marathon. It's an easy message to remember but a difficult one to commit our lives to.

The results are worth the wait. Those smaller plants—something like a tomato plant—are lucky to produce twenty pounds of tomatoes in a given season. The apple tree can produce hundreds of pounds of fruit.

You may witness small plants popping up all around you. Know that God is pruning, seasoning, and preparing you for His work in His way.

—⁊⁊⁊—

Apply Today's Truth

- Is there a particular area of your life in which you've become impatient with God? What causes these feelings?
- In what ways does God show patience with you?

28

Investing

*The plans of the diligent lead to profit as surely
as haste leads to poverty.
—Proverbs 21:5 (NIV)*

The topic of investing can be a confusing one. Mention the phrase *investing in the stock market,* and prepare for a wild swing of emotional reactions.

Some people will shout out their exuberance and thrill for the market and wonder why everyone isn't right there with them. *How are you not investing everything in these particular hot stocks?*

The other crowd is huddled in the fetal position in the corner wondering how anyone could ever sign up to experience the wild ride of the market. *How can you stand all the ups and downs?*

Let's understand a couple of things up front. Investing is just like every other aspect of your financial life. Remember first, "the earth is the Lord's and everything in it." (Psalm 24:1 NIV) Every account, every stock, every bond, every investment is meant to serve and glorify God. It's still His money. We must treat it as such.

Second, investing should only be considered after achieving some of the other principles we've already discussed. Make sure you've saved enough for emergencies. Have your debt eliminated or be working on the plan to make that happen. Consider investing with your surplus of funds.

There is risk associated with investing your money, but that doesn't make it wrong. It just means you better have a plan of action in place before taking action. Proverbs 14:15 (NIV) advises prudence. "A simple man believes anything, but a prudent man gives thought to his steps."

You must consider several things before opening an investment account. Why are you even thinking about investing? Is this money you'll be depending on to provide income in the next five years, fifteen years, or thirty years? Are you trying to grow a certain account for the purpose of leaving it for your family later?

Your need for the funds and your time of life affect the type of investment risk you should consider. Are you looking for a more aggressive or more conservative portfolio?

Either way, don't get caught up in the adrenalin of the market. Take a deep breath and understand that investing should be considered a long-term activity without the pipe dream of getting rich quickly. "Dishonest money dwindles away, but he who gathers money little by little makes it grow." (Proverbs 13:11 NIV) I encourage all my clients that a slow-and-steady attitude wins the race whether we're dealing with aggressive or conservative risk tolerance.

The Bible speaks on another key to investing wisely. Solomon discussed the importance of diversification in Ecclesiastes 11:2 (NIV). "Give portions to seven, yes to eight, for you do not know what disaster may come upon the land."

The only certainty when dealing with the economy is uncertainty. No one knows what tomorrow will bring. Solomon's argument here is while that may be true, it doesn't mean we should sit around doing nothing.

Look back at Matthew 25:14-30 in the parable of the loaned money. Each servant was given a different number of talents to care for when the master went away. The first two servants worked and gained more. They doubled what they had been entrusted with. The servant with one talent dug a hole and stuck it in the ground. The master did not reward him for safely guarding that one coin. He scolded him for not working to increase what he had. He was called wicked and lazy.

We are called to oversee and wisely increase what we've been given as a steward of God's provision. Don't just stick your head in the sand because you don't know any better or you're scared. It's not your fault if you find yourself in that position, but you do become culpable if you don't work to move forward with the instructions you've been given.

Proverbs 15:22 (NIV) addresses this exact situation. "Plans fail for lack of counsel, but with many advisers they succeed." It's your job to seek information and helpful people. It doesn't mean everyone is looking out for your best interests. That's where godly discernment comes into play.

Look to professionals you have a relationship with. Ask family and friends for referrals of who's helping them with investing their retirement funds and creating their financial plans. Seek out advisors with certain credentials. I obtained the Certified Kingdom Advisor® designation for this very reason. I want folks to know what I stand for and how I operate.

Interview multiple people before making a decision. Ask tough questions and get the answers you need before moving forward. You're never going to understand every aspect of investing in the beginning. That's why you must find someone you trust to help you make tremendously important decisions.

If you're applying biblical advice on how to grow your money over time, you'll be able to take the emotion out of investing. Make a plan, have a long-term mindset, diversify your portfolio, and remember, it's all God's. "For God did not give us a spirit of timidity, but a spirit of power, of love, and of self-discipline." (2 Timothy 1:7 NIV)

We can't know what the future holds, but we can know the One who holds the future as Christian investors.[16]

—◦◦◦—

Apply Today's Truth

- Are you currently investing in the stock market? If so, have you developed a plan to dictate your risk level, amount of money invested, and determined the need for each account? Providing good answers to these questions can help you see if you're investing according to God's plan.

- If you've always been nervous about investing, I encourage you to spend time in prayer to see how God wants to lead you. Do you need to stick to the safety of guaranteed financial products, or would it help to seek out a trusted professional to help you on your journey? Investing in the stock market is not the correct answer for everyone.

29

Receiving God's Blessings

*What I'm trying to do here is get you to relax,
not be so preoccupied with "getting"
so you can respond to God's "giving".*
—*Luke 12:29 (MSG)*

It seems when I focus on receiving, I often miss what God is trying to give me. How often do I rob God an opportunity of giving to me? I only pay attention to what's directly in front of me. I see Options A and B while God is planning Option C in a way that makes no sense whatsoever to my finite brain. And then when it happens I think, wow, how did that occur?

I arrived at a crossroads in my life several years ago, unhappy with my current role, while being given an opportunity to change paths. The problem was it meant returning to an industry I had already decided to move out of a few years previous for numerous reasons. I didn't want to return, but it seemed better than where I was.

I spent several days unable to make a decision because neither one was a desirable choice. I found myself praying for the answer to *my* question—should I remain at Job A or take Job B? At no time did I consider asking God to simply guide me toward *His* will. I could only see *my* two options.

The day came to make a decision, and I received a phone call that changed everything. It was an opportunity to further my current career in a new environment with another company which included a better opportunity for growth and an increase in salary and potential. I had never spoken with this employer before, and the call seemingly came out of the blue. I was floored.

We fail to understand that God is never surprised and never looks up to proclaim, "Well, I didn't see that coming!" He purposefully makes it difficult for us to understand when something so good happens in our lives. He reveals these things in amazing ways so we have no choice but to look at Him, acknowledge His involvement and His kindness, and thank Him for it all.

I know how often I push forward with a decision when my "gut" tells me not to. What does my "gut" feeling really represent? I believe the Holy Spirit communicates with us in a myriad of ways. He lets us know when something is just flat-out wrong. Honestly, it's usually not too hard to recognize.

There are other times when something just doesn't feel right. We can't confuse that feeling with simply not wanting to feel uncomfortable. One of our Father's main objectives is to force us out of our safety zones. When we experience discomfort, it forces us to make a move. Otherwise, we'd never grow.

Sometimes at work, I'm facing a decision that might actually produce a good outcome either way I choose, but for some reason, I'm just uneasy about moving forward in a certain direction. The particular option might make sense to me, but God tells me "No."

It might even be a decision that would benefit someone else in the same situation. I can't focus on that. I must be sensitive to listening for God's voice. Is God telling me this isn't the path I need to travel right now? But I still question Him. It seems like the smart choice. Look at how well that other person is doing. Has God ever spoken directly to you and told you to knock it off? "It doesn't matter what the other person is doing. I'm telling you what *you* need to do."

It's your choice how to respond to God. Your flesh will claim it knows better. You've been here before. Why are you even questioning your own feelings and experiences? You must remember God's thoughts are higher than your thoughts and His ways higher than your ways (Isaiah 55:8-9).

He desires for you to live your life more abundantly. This doesn't mean you'll always be rich in the earthly sense. That's prosperity gospel junk. What it does mean is you'll experience an increase in your desire to know Him and to understand Him. You'll find yourself making time to spend with His Word instead of making excuses as to why you shouldn't.

"But whoever looks intently into the perfect law that gives freedom, and continues in it—not forgetting what they have heard, but doing it—they will be blessed in what they do" (James 1:25 NIV).

God cares for you individually and desires for you to connect with Him with your mind, your body, and your soul. You're ready and listening. You're prepared to respond to God appropriately by saying what's happening doesn't make sense based on what you know, but thankfully you've got Him to lead you.

"So we do not lose heart. Though our outer self is wasting away, our inner self is being renewed day by day. For this light momentary affliction is preparing for us an eternal weight of glory beyond all comparison, as we look not to the things that are seen but to the things that are unseen. For the things that are seen are transient, but the things that are unseen are eternal" (2 Corinthians 4:16-18 ESV).

If you can successfully live your life with this kind of connection to the One and Only Savior of the universe, you are preparing yourself to receive His blessings and everything He has in store for you. It is reassuring when you continue to rely on Him. Train your mind and your thoughts to love Him, trust Him, and to quit doubting Him in future situations.

Apply Today's Truth

- Can you recognize times in your life when you've made a bad decision because you relied too heavily on your own way of thinking rather than surrendering to God's?
- Are you prepared to receive the blessings of God? You must learn to trust and obey Him even when His instructions don't make total sense to you at the time. Pray for the strength to follow through with obedience.

30

Find Wise Mentors

*My son, keep your father's command
and do not forsake your mother's teaching.
Bind them always on your heart; fasten them around
your neck. When you walk, they will guide you;
when you sleep, they will watch over you;
when you awake, they will speak to you.*
—Proverbs 6:20-22 (NIV)

When I was a little boy, my parents made a small investment, probably five to ten bucks, that established the foundation of financial principles that guides nearly every decision I have made with money since that time.

It was the Winkin' George Bank. A small piggy bank with George Washington's picture from the $1 bill plastered in the top center part of it. There was a coin slot at the top. It held $17.50—a perfect roll of pennies, nickels, dimes and quarters. All of the change I collected headed straight into this bank.

The premier feature of this contraption was our founding father would wink at you every time you placed a coin in the top slot, and it rolled magically into the appropriate column of coins.

I worked feverishly to fill those coin rolls up as quickly as possible. Because when I did... we sealed those coin rolls and took them to the now former Southtrust Bank, where I would deposit $10 into my savings account and received $7.50 for my personal use.

This was the early 1980s. Seven bucks could still get you some cool things as a kid. I forget what those earliest purchases were with my new money, but it didn't take long before I was searching for baseball card packs to start a new hobby that I still participate in today.

What were my parents doing? They were forming a mindset inside my young brain. Anytime I received money, I needed to consider saving some of it. I didn't know they were teaching me this. Honestly, at the time, I didn't really understand why I couldn't spend all of the money. It was mine.

Don't get the wrong idea. We weren't rolling in the dough. My parents worked hard and sacrificed royally for my sister and me, but we were not a rich family. If we were middle class, we barely made the cut. That's not a knock on my parents' efforts at all. It's just the truth.

But my mom and dad still understood it was crucial to teach me a valuable life lesson. I needed to implement a habit of putting back a little bit whenever possible every single payday. Today, my wife and I are adamant about paying off debt, saving for retirement, and giving more when we receive more. I know a large portion of my current habits were formed by the lessons my parents taught me almost forty years ago.

Look at how their contributions affected my life. I now lead other families through financial instruction. You're reading a book I wrote about handling your finances in a biblical way. All of this didn't occur by coincidence. God knew exactly what would be happening at this point of my life even before I left my mother's womb. This was part of His perfect master plan.

His plan produces divine ways to match us with parents, family, and wise counsel throughout our years. He's dropping off tidbits and ideas along the way so we'll learn a little at a time. He wants us to take the knowledge, just like with His Word, think about it, ponder it, hold it close to our hearts, and then apply it to our daily lives.

Even as adults, don't neglect to seek wise counsel in your life. You may not have the best relationship with your parents. They may not be the best financial role models. You can still glean from some of their money adventures.

I've learned when giving advice to people, sometimes the most helpful advice is to discourage someone from making a move they shouldn't make. Learn from other people's mistakes, and don't make the same one.

Maybe your parents shared a story of learning a lesson after the fact. Now they realize they might've spent a little more than they should have at the time. They recognize the more expensive vehicle or the bigger house was more than what was really needed. It caused a problematic situation they could've avoided.

Their experiences can absolutely serve to enlighten you as well. You witness how their bad decisions led to a time of concern and money getting tight. Obviously, you shouldn't fall into the same trap. A lesson like that can save you years of misery, worry, and fear with your own finances.

Go to your pastor or church leaders and ask to talk to someone they trust about doing money God's way. I cannot imagine they wouldn't try to do everything possible to help guide you toward a godly decision-making process. I've included resources in the back of this book to help you as well.

And please don't forget the whole purpose of this book is to make sure you're studying the teachings of our heavenly Father and His practical advice toward your everyday living. There are over 2,000 verses that deal with helpful Scripture aimed at you making decisions to please God. Pick up the Bible, and let the Holy Spirit breathe into you.

Listen to those who can teach you. Discern their wise counsel. Keep it in mind and never forget it. Let the wisdom guide you, protect you, and teach you throughout your journey.

—⁓—

Apply Today's Truth

- Can you identify people in your life who are living out God's stewardship principles that might be willing to mentor you?
- What lessons have you learned from your parents about dealing with your finances?

31

Raising a Good Steward

Start children off on the way they should go,
and even when they are old they will not turn from it.
—Proverbs 22:6 (NIV)

I honestly cannot imagine growing up as a teenager during these times. I reflect on the pressures I experienced back in the 1990s as I entered high school, transitioned to college, and then took the leap into adulthood. I see my teenage daughter beginning her college career with all the same pressures but with a host of new ones added to the list.

The constant onslaught of social media and information attacking her from every angle imaginable is a difficult task for any child to endure. It overwhelms many adults today as well. I know there are a lot of folks my age who are tremendously thankful social media didn't arrive until those early parts of life were completed. I can hear the chorus of "Amens" from all of you in my age group and above.

The amount of messaging and communication we're exposed to is mind boggling. Consider text messaging. For something not even possible three decades ago, Americans now send over six billion texts every day—a total of over twenty-seven trillion texts each year.[17] Our country is responsible for originating 45 percent of the world's text messages.

If you thought it was difficult hearing and sorting out the Lord's message above all the noise three decades ago, take a minute to let those numbers sink in. I didn't even mention the thousands of television channels, music formats, and podcasts available and fighting for our kids' attention. The worst part of it is children hold the capability of access to all this information in their hands right now.

As parents, it is more imperative than ever before that we intentionally stress to our children the information they need to hear. We must be diligent in steering them to the message of God if they have any chance of establishing a spiritual life in Christ.

It's no secret our culture loudly proclaims the importance of living a narcissistic lifestyle and taking advantage of unlimited choices in the market. They're hearing the mixed messages, and they're sticking. A study performed by psychologists at Purdue University in 2018 showed kids begin to grasp basic money concepts by age three. Just four years later, many of their money habits are already set.[18]

Do not slack off from your responsibility of teaching and training your children in financial literacy. Whether you believe it or not, your habits and your words still hold a great deal of influence over their thinking.

"These commandments that I give you today are to be on your hearts. Impress them on your children. Talk about them when you sit at home and when you walk along the road, when you lie down and when you get up" (Deuteronomy 6:6-7 NIV).

Ron Blue covers this topic in his teachings. He lists four skills kids must master to learn money God's way:[19]

- How to develop a spending plan
- How to buy wisely
- How to make financial decisions
- How to set financial goals

We can achieve these skills in a variety of ways while considering the ages of each child. The important things to remember are for the child to personally experience the lesson. They should be responsible (with appropriate parameters) for making money decisions while also having the opportunity to fail. We must be willing to give feedback and reward them for correct behavior.

You can use envelope systems to separate categories. We've tried the three jars process for our girls— one to give, one to spend, one to save. The rules are set for how their weekly allowance is divvied up. We allow them to make their own choices for extra money earned during the weeks.

For older kids, Christy and I tried an idea last Christmas with my oldest daughter Emma for the first time. We gave her a gift of money but included a letter informing her it wasn't for her to spend on herself. Our directions explained she was to research and decide on a charity performing kingdom work to receive the funds and then explain to us the reasons behind her choice. She chose to donate to an organization she participated with during an international school mission trip. Those dollars helped provide clean water for a poor neighborhood in need. This is a lesson we'll use again in the future with her and her younger sisters.

My girls don't see me at my upstairs desk sending our tithe to the church, paying bills, or saving to our retirement accounts. I do everything on my computer. All the more reason our leadership in teaching them is vital.

Use some creativity. Think of ways you can teach your children based on your family's interests and how you typically handle money. Be transparent to a certain point with your kids. They don't need to know everything about your finances.

If you've made great decisions or horrible mistakes, share those stories with them. It helps more than you know to show your human side. You are not perfect, but you have valuable experiences to pass on to them.

Our kids need to learn the same things we did as we moved into our independent adult years. There is no get-rich-quick method available to teach. The secret formula still involves hard work and putting in the time.

Recall all the lessons you've already studied throughout this book. Don't you think there's some valuable information you can share with them?

Start them early.

Anything they learn and retain regarding God's principles of stewardship will play a significant role in establishing the foundation of their future financial wisdom.

———

Apply Today's Truth

- Have you ever discussed money with your children? Gather some ideas from Christian sources and determine what ideas you can initiate to begin their learning process.
- Lift your children up through constant prayer concerning their decisions. Help show them how God is available for all who seek His advice, including them.

32

Heavenly Expectations

For we are God's handiwork,
created in Christ Jesus to do good works,
which God prepared in advance for us to do.
—Ephesians 2:10 (NIV)

So then, each of us will give an account
of ourselves to God.
—Romans 14:12 (NIV)

Everything we've discussed and studied throughout this book is predicated on the fact we're shifting our attention to an eternal perspective and away from the temporary realm of this world. The Bible demonstrates our rewards for doing so include developing a more intimate relationship with Jesus. We increase our desire to please Him while fulfilling His purpose for our existence.

Remember, our stewardship activities have no bearing on our *admittance* to heaven. Our salvation is strictly based on the grace of God and our faith in the death, resurrection, and reign of His Son, Jesus Christ, as our Savior (Ephesians 2:8-9).

The spiritual fruit we produce, however, absolutely impacts how we spend our time in eternity with Christ. Our good works make a larger impact than you may think on how we experience heaven. In Revelation 22:12 (NIV), Jesus exclaims, "Look, I am coming soon! My reward is with me, and I will give to each person according to what they have done." Our opportunities will be based on our established record before we arrive.

Heaven is a magnificent place for everyone who resides there, and I pray you've made the decision necessary to reserve your spot. As a Christian, you are assured of your eternity there. You'll never face condemnation, but Jesus promises, in Romans 14:12, we will all face an evaluation of our performance against His expectations for our lives. We see this promise again in 2 Corinthians 5:10 (NIV). "For we must all appear before the judgment seat of Christ, so that each of us may receive what is due us for the things done while in the body, whether good or bad."

God will ask you about all those opportunities wasted every time you decided you were too busy or simply chose to go your own way. You are created and called to do the work of the Lord. You are designed to make a difference in the kingdom with the spiritual gifts and responsibilities assigned to you. The ultimate act of stewardship is using your life to serve God and others.

The Bible speaks of the heavenly rewards and special privileges available to us.[20]

- Imperishable Crown—1 Corinthians 9:24-25—living a disciplined life
- Crown of Rejoicing—1 Thessalonians 2:19—dedication to evangelism and discipleship
- Crown of Righteousness—2 Timothy 4:8—living obediently while waiting for Christ's return
- Crown of Life—James 1:12—persevering through trials without denying Christ
- Crown of Glory—1 Peter 5:4—serving as church leader in a way that pleased God

Some other special treatments mentioned in Scripture include receiving a rich welcome from Jesus in heaven (2 Peter 1:11) and being allowed special access to the Tree of Life (Revelation 2:7).

Keep these crowns and rewards in mind when you're tempted to allow your self-centeredness to get in the way of serving God now. It's easy to believe nobody notices your diligent ministry work. It's true people around you may miss your good deeds, but your heavenly Father sees absolutely everything. The small things you do for others will count highly for you in glory. Let this be an encouragement for when frustration starts to set in.

Paul instructs us, in Hebrews 12:1-4, to throw off sin and everything else that tries to stop us from serving God. We must persevere in our faith and set our eyes solely on Him. If we shift our focus and concentrate elsewhere, we are guaranteed to sink into the deep water.

Peter lost his focus and began to drop quickly (Matthew 14:29-30) before locking eyes again with Christ. Then Jesus reached out His hand to save him. Paul tells us to fight hard against the forces of opposition and to remember what Jesus did for us. Only His strength allows us to endure, not grow weary, and not lose heart.

The way we think about heaven and what our responsibilities will be there have a huge impact on the decisions we make in our present time. Do not allow yourself to believe some of the many misperceptions of what spending eternity in heaven actually means. Our main priority will be worshiping God and fulfilling His will just like we do now. The great thing missing will be the sin and evil that are so prevalent in our current world.

We know everything good comes from God. Expect to live in an abundance of joy when we're with Him. We will be reunited with loved ones. We will serve God with our spiritual gifts. It will be endless amounts of continuous praise and worship.

But we must start our preparation now. Knowing His Word, understanding His Word, living out His Word; we have our marching orders. We know what needs to be done. Christian pastor and author Dr. Robert Jeffress sums up this lesson well. "The more seriously we take heaven, the more seriously we'll take earth."[21] Make up your mind today to fulfill your heavenly expectations.

———∽∽∼———

Apply Today's Truth

- Have you given much thought to preparing yourself for your days in heaven?
- Do you understand your time of judgment and what needs to be done here on earth to be ready for that day?

V

Giving by God's Standards

33

Surrendering Your Worldly Goods

And they exceeded our expectations:
They gave themselves first of all to the Lord,
and then by the will of God also to us.
—*2 Corinthians 8:5 (NIV)*

Talk about coming through in the clutch. Even in the midst of extreme poverty throughout the land, the Macedonian churches located in Philippi, Thessalonica, and Berea made it happen. They even amazed Paul... and this is a man who experienced some pretty incredible miracles delivered straight from God. It's safe to assume he wasn't easily impressed.

Despite the horrible circumstances and another unnamed severe trial, the Macedonians blew the doors off the church fundraiser. They gave beyond their own ability. How does that even work? The people—get this—"urgently pleaded" with Paul and his team for the privilege to take part in this collection.

Have you ever heard someone in the congregation urgently plead to the ushers to send the offering plates back around the room one more time? Just because those in attendance were begging to give more? I don't think so.

What causes this nonsensical behavior? The absolute supernatural power of Jesus.

Here's the key to how all this came together. Look what happened in 2 Corinthians 8:5. "They gave themselves first of all to the Lord, and then by the will of God also to [Paul and his team]."

They gave themselves first to the Lord. Hard to tap into supernatural power if the Lord isn't leading the way. You can't pull off these miracles by yourself.

I think the better point to drive home in this Scripture is the fact you cannot find the actual amount the churches gave. Today we're posting those numbers (especially if they're splendid) in the church bulletin, the weekly email, and all of the church's social media outlets. Sometimes we even post a large banner or that gigantic thermometer poster to help track our progress.

But no, the actual totals are nowhere to be found. Why is that? Because God doesn't care. The number doesn't matter to Him. He could've whipped up every last penny needed for the project if He'd wanted to. Remember what He did with five barley loaves and two small fish?

The important thing here was a whole group of people down on their luck, unable to purchase the necessities, much less anything extra for their own families, came together and gave themselves first to the Lord. What an awesome picture of everything God is trying to teach us throughout His entire Scripture!

I can imagine God saying, "If you all would just bow the knee, acknowledge My kingdom, and ask Me to guide you, you would be amazed at what I could do!"

Ever been told it doesn't matter what you say, but how you say it? In this case, it doesn't necessarily matter what you did, it's how and why you did it. Jesus cares about your soul. He cares about your focus, your attitude, and your intent.

These folks declared it didn't matter how bad their current circumstances were. They relied on the leadership of Paul who was allowing his ministry to be directed solely by God. They proclaimed joy in the midst of hard living and horrible financial conditions. If God says He can still use me in this condition, then I'm all in.

Proclaiming that particular message is not an easy declaration to make. It is a requirement to already have a sturdy foundation in place to walk the path. It's not often you see the words "overflowing joy" to describe those in "extreme poverty" that leads to a "rich generosity." Supernatural power causes supernatural results.

It doesn't make any sense to our feeble brains and our limited power of understanding. What does make sense is God proving His Word is true. Be content, have a heart full of giving. Then stand back and watch God do God things.

Paul is sharing this story in his letter to the Corinthians. They too were experiencing some tough times, but they had come a long way recently in their spiritual maturation. Their folks were building their faith, developing strong teaching, and loving each other, but they needed some help in learning how to give. Don't we all?

Here we see Paul encouraging, not commanding, the Corinthians to adopt the same attitude. But don't do it just because I'm asking you to, do it because you know and love your Father. Do it because of what Jesus Himself did for every one of us. "For God so loved the world…" (John 3:16).

Since God loved, we're expected to love as well. This is how the kingdom grows. If each one of us decided to love each other and give sacrificially, think of how different this world could be. Can you imagine having to form a church committee to decide how to spend all the surplus funds because the congregation literally begged to give as much as they could? Why is that question such a preposterous one? Why isn't it happening in every church?

It's a heart thing. It's not a resource thing. These Macedonian believers proved as much. They couldn't make a big difference individually. You may not be able to either. However, what little you give can be added to what little your brothers and sisters give. Before long, you're all gathered in the name of God. Lives are changed and the name of Jesus is proclaimed and praised in a world longing to see, hear, and experience a little good news.

—⁓—

Apply Today's Truth

- Identify a part of your life you need to surrender to God. You may be giving to Him in many different ways. Where are you holding back to keep some for yourself?
- Ask God to help you realize how much He wants you to participate in His kingdom work. Satan will attempt to use your weaknesses against you. Pray for God to direct you to your assigned mission field.

34

The Blessing of Tithing

"Bring the whole tithe into the storehouse, that there may be food in my house. Test me in this," says the LORD Almighty, "and see if I will not throw open the floodgates of heaven and pour out so much blessing that there will not be room enough to store it."
—*Malachi 3:10 (NIV)*

We work hard, day in and day out. Up at the crack of dawn, back home after dark. We give so much to our careers so we can take care of our families, afford a nice place to live, put food on the table, and maybe have a little left over to save or spend on some fun stuff.

It's not a natural inclination for us to offer to give away a good chunk of our hard-earned paycheck. Are you crazy? I worked hard for that money. I deserve it.

No, it's not a natural feeling. The last time I checked, God doesn't hang out in the *natural* field of play. He deals more with the *supernatural*.

If we imply we're living a Christian life, full of Christian values and ideas, then we're going to need to act like it. God doesn't simply ask us for a few hours on Sunday morning every week. He commands a larger commitment.

That's because He provided us with *everything*. Our problem is we believe we're *giving up* 10 percent (as a minimum) of our money to please God.

God is responsible for everything we have, everything we achieve, every blessing in our lives. He reminds us of this by asking us to simply live on most of what He provides. We're able to show our thankfulness to Him by setting aside some of those gifts to give back to Him and His kingdom.

Let's get one thing straight—God does not need our money to achieve *anything*. What He asks of us is actually a tremendously gracious gesture on His part. Think about any time you've done something for someone when you gave of yourself, your time, or your resources in a sacrificial way. I'm talking about giving without expecting anything in return.

What was the result of your giving? Aren't you usually blessed ten-fold above and beyond the person you were actually trying to bless? You've experienced God's supernatural work. Our heavenly Father allows us to be useful for His kingdom. My sinful, dirty, flesh-abiding human self... able to make a difference in the kingdom of God. Unreal.

In Malachi 3:10, God is instructing the people to bring the whole tithe into the storehouse. Don't cheat me, because I know when you do. And then He says something He doesn't say anywhere else in the Bible. "Test me in this". Whoa. Think back to when Satan tempted Jesus in the gospels. Christ restated a verse from Deuteronomy 6:16 (NIV): "Do not put the Lord your God to the test." Malachi is the one place in Scripture where God says, "I dare you. Trust me on this one."

And it comes with a promise. If you test God by giving as He instructs you to, He will "throw open the floodgates of heaven and pour out so much blessing that there will not be room enough to store it." Don't get confused here. God's not promising you earthly riches for obeying Him. He may choose to go that route, and that's His prerogative.

But what He will do is bless you in ways you cannot imagine. You won't even receive the best of those rewards until you're living in eternity with Him.

"But store up for yourselves treasures in heaven, where moths and vermin do not destroy, and where thieves do not break in and steal" (Matthew 6:20 NIV).

As we grow, we learn more and more about our faith. It doesn't surprise me that new Christians might have a hard time with the idea of giving back 10 percent of their income to Christ. But as we mature, our focus and perspective should start reflecting, and then changing, the way we think about and deal with Jesus in our lives.

The things that used to be "I have to do" become "I get to do." I look back at my thoughts years ago, and I couldn't imagine giving 10 percent of my *gross* income to God. Believe me, it took me a while to move there from giving from the actual amount I saw in my paycheck. I discovered motivation when my pastor told a story about being asked frequently which amount we should give.

His response? What part of your income would you like God to bless? Your net income or *all* your income.

Now, my wife and I are searching for ways to give more. Our goal is to make sure we give away much more than 10 percent of our income every year. We're finding new ways to share our values and our giving with our children. Hopefully, they'll understand sooner than we did how important this concept is. We already see progress in all our girls' attitudes.

Were we blessed before we started tithing?

Absolutely.

Are we convinced the blessings multiplied once we obeyed God's command to give Him our first fruits? Without a doubt. It's a part of our spiritual maturity just like any other growth area in our lives.

The couple of verses before Malachi 3:10 actually reveal what we're really doing when we disobey this command. We're robbing God.[22] We can only believe it when we're able to honestly admit we're not dealing with our stuff. It's all God's. And it's perfectly acceptable for Him to ask us to give as He sees fit.

His whole relationship with us is based on us trusting Him, and in knowing He is who He says He is. He is almighty. He is all loving. He is all giving. If we can't realize the truth, then there's something wrong with our relationship with Him in the first place.

When we give, we are supplying our ministers, our churches, and our missions with the money God created for them to use to expand the kingdom of God. We're doing our part. We're pleasing God with our actions.

The blessings will overflow, and God will leave you no doubt you were created to give.

—◦◦◦—

Apply Today's Truth

- If you have not yet made the decision to start tithing, it's time to figure out why not. Tithing is a non-negotiable when it comes to living a true Christian lifestyle. God does not suggest tithing; He commands it.

- If you have committed to tithing, how else is God instructing you to give?

35

Be a Cheerful Giver

*If I give all I possess to the poor and give
over my body to hardship that I may boast,
but do not have love, I gain nothing.*
—*1 Corinthians 13:3 (NIV)*

Why do we give? What's our motive? It's not natural to want to give away what is ours. Our sinful flesh rejects the idea outright. We are made selfish and self-centered.

Watch two small kids playing with a toy they both enjoy. It doesn't take long until one is snatching it from the other or using their own body to shield the other child from being able to take it away. I see this in my own home often. My wife and I don't have to teach our girls to be greedy.

The instinct is already there.

We're forced to sometimes reach for extreme measures to stress the need for kindness and sharing our possessions with each other. It's not an easy character trait to teach or to learn.

God knew this. He sent His Son to earth to save us from our destructive behavior and decision making. John 3:16 (NIV) tells us everything we need to know.

"For God so loved the world that He gave His one and only Son, that whoever believes in Him shall not perish but have eternal life."

There's all the proof we need to understand how much God loves His people. He knew exactly why Jesus was needed.

His death didn't just happen after He took human form for a few years. God didn't run into a problem He didn't see coming, ponder over His options, and decide sacrificing His Son was probably the best way to achieve what He needed to accomplish.

God knew from the beginning of time. He knew our hearts would be dark and sour, filled with sin, and unable to congregate with Him in a perfect heaven.

He can't associate with sin. So, God decided to do the absolute unthinkable.

He reached into His heart and formed a Savior that would bear the brunt of our wickedness all the way to Calvary.

We've witnessed the type of giving we're called to do. No, we're not asked to send our children to their deaths for people who don't even like us. Even though that's exactly what God did for us.

We are commanded to give generously and with self-sacrifice.

How do we know we're giving like we're designed to do? I've heard folks tell me to give until it hurts.

My favorite response to that statement is:

"Don't give until it hurts, give until it feels good."   —Dennis Kimbro[23]

That's when you know you're doing it right.

If we're living in the will of the Almighty, we will actively search for ways to give. We'll have our antenna up and our binoculars pointed outwards to find our next suspect. It might be paying for someone's lunch, helping lighten someone's load, or simply giving a word of encouragement. There's no end to the possibilities.

If you're growing in your walk with Jesus, getting closer to Him every day, your every desire will start turning away from yourself and point toward someone who could surely use a blessing.

Our overall financial situation is directly affected by the depth of our intimacy with God. When we start thinking more and more like Christ, we're far less likely to run up the credit card bill on frivolous things we don't really need.

I've been driving a car that's now ten years old. My wife's even encouraged me to find something new, but I'm just not motivated to make the change and spend the extra money on a vehicle I really don't currently need. This one still runs perfectly, it's safe, and it still takes me everywhere I need to go. The desire just isn't there. I'd rather save the money, and spend it on our family or someone else.

I'm no saint when it comes to being thrifty with our cash. I still have hobbies and activities I spend way too much on. I'm sure it's only a matter of time until the Lord begins working on those things. He just knows I can only handle a few growth areas at a time.

Remember it's a heart thing with God. He doesn't even want us going through the motions of giving if it's only for show or because we feel like we have to.

Check out what Paul said in 2 Corinthians 9:7 (NLT). "You must decide in your heart how much to give. And don't give reluctantly or in response to pressure. For God loves a person who gives cheerfully."

God loves a cheerful giver. He makes it pretty easy to understand. If you're not giving with a cheerful heart, a grateful heart, a warm heart, don't even bother giving. It's not going to be blessed by Him.

God does not honor giving with the wrong attitude.

If you can't be grateful for all God has given to you and want to share it, why are you even going through the motions? To check a box? To say you did it for others to know and see? God doesn't want or need your money.

Our lives have become so much more enjoyable since we've started looking for ways to give away more money. We don't say yes to every single opportunity which comes along, or we'd quickly spend everything God's given us to raise our family and prepare for our future. But we give a lot more than we used to, because we want to.

We now have the desire to give.

My wife and I are happier and more fulfilled when we do. We'd like to teach our kids how to do the same thing, so when they actually have their own money, they'll want to give when it's completely their own decision.

God gave to us because He loves us. He expects us to follow His perfect example. We should desire to give because of our love for Him and for His people.

———∽∾∽———

Apply Today's Truth

- What kind of attitude do you have when you give your tithe or other offerings? Are you hesitant to do so? Pray for God to guide you through those feelings to a place of awareness and gratitude.
- Be aware of opportunities to bless others as God directs you. He will provide opportunities throughout your day and week if you're in tune with Him and paying attention.

36

Generosity Is More Than Money

Command them to do good, to be rich in good deeds,
and to be generous and willing to share.
—1 Timothy 6:18 (NIV)

I can see the eyes of church members rolling upwards as they've just been told the pastor was embarking on a series of sermons focused on stewardship. "Here we go again. They must be asking for money for something. What are we building now?" You know exactly what I'm talking about.

The church definition of stewardship is often talked about and thought about in relation only to money. As, hopefully, you've realized after reading most of this book, nothing could be further from the truth.

We are responsible for giving to others through a multitude of different gifts God has bestowed upon our lives.

Billy Graham spoke about this subject when he said, "Where do we get the notion that our idea of success and God's are the same? You have written a book; you are a clever manager and promoter; you are a talented artist; you are independently wealthy; you have achieved fame and fortune. Without the gifts of intelligence, imagination, personality, and physical energy—which are all endowed by God—where would you be?"[24]

You may not feel like it sometimes, but you are created by God with gifts galore. The things you know, the way you act, the energy you receive from your beating heart—God has a plan and an opportunity for every single one of those gifts.

"But since you excel in everything—in faith, in speech, in knowledge, in complete earnestness and in the love we have kindled in you— see that you also excel in this grace of giving" (2 Corinthians 8:7 NIV).

God expects you to take care of the life and the light He's entrusted in you and to share it with others. He provides you with an abundance of joy. Don't you believe someone who doesn't know Christ could use that same joy?

It is your responsibility to share it with someone who so desperately needs it. "Let your light shine before others, that they may see your good deeds and glorify your Father in heaven" (Matthew 5:16 NIV).

The very vessel God chose for you is not an accident. Your body is a gift to steward just like the money in your wallet is. In 1 Corinthians 6:19-20 (NIV), Paul makes it clear we should take care of ourselves physically, mentally, and spiritually. "Do you not know that your bodies are temples of the Holy Spirit, who is in you, whom you have received from God? You are not your own; you were bought at a price. Therefore honor God with your bodies."

We've discussed many times how your money is not yours, but God's. Your body is not yours either. It is owned by God. It is on loan to you. As a Christian, you are housing the exact same Holy Spirit who swept across the earth and led thousands of people to a life in Christ during the earliest days of the church (Acts 2:1-4, 38-41).

God has entrusted the Holy Spirit to you so you can give your money, your time, and yourself to the work of His kingdom for as long as He decides you need to stick around. If God still has you breathing (which I'm assuming is the case if you're reading this), you still have purpose.

You still have a need to properly care for the body He's given you. Concentrate on what goes into your body in the form of nutrition and harmful substances. Staying healthy must remain a priority. It's hard to work and persevere for the Savior if you're dealing with health issues you could've avoided by making better decisions along the way. I know full well you're not totally in control of how you physically and mentally hold up over time, but you should be faithful in affecting the parts you can.

We're each given the exact same amount of time every day. You have 1,440 minutes to plan out seven days a week. It's up to us to use it in a godly way. Of course, certain things have to be scheduled, but how are you planning the time outside of work and other commitments?

Do you need to investigate what those other commitments are?

"We need to be energetically at work for the One who sent me here, working while the sun shines. When night falls, the workday is over" (John 9:4 MSG).

"Use your heads as you live and work among outsiders. Don't miss a trick. Make the most of every opportunity" (Colossians 4:5 MSG).

"The world and its desires pass away, but whoever does the will of God lives forever" (1 John 2:17 NIV).

Our time is precious. We have no idea when we'll be called to Heaven or when Jesus will return to retrieve all His followers. The time we have remaining must be spent wisely with a concentration on His work assigned to us.

I've discovered in recent years the more I search for ways to spend time working for God, the more time He seems to create for me to get everything done. It's really difficult to explain. He's continued to bless me in unbelievable ways during periods of my life when

I've fully committed to His chosen projects at the correct time.

I took a step of faith in those instances because I didn't understand how I would be able to complete His task while still taking care of my commitments involving family, career, and church. But He just keeps proving His faithfulness every time I try giving back His gifts for His use.

I urge you to do the same and experience the awesomeness of our God. Give Him your time. Give Him your characteristics. Give Him your personality. Give Him your physical self. Give Him every single thing that makes you, well, you.

—*ww*—

Apply Today's Truth

- Do you have trouble identifying God's gifts in the way you were made? Please ask Him to reveal the special ways He's designed you to fulfill His purpose for your life.
- Reflect on how your time is spent. This is an easy gift to waste. There are so many ways to fill our schedules with things that just don't matter eternally. Explore how you can better serve God with your time.

37

Discipline Yourself to Give

*Train yourself for godliness; for while bodily
training is of some value, godliness is of value
in every way, as it holds promise for the present life
and also for the life to come.*
—*1 Timothy 4:7-8 (ESV)*

College football is a big deal in my part of the world. It's discussed on television, radio, and around the office year-round. I love the excitement and pageantry of gameday and being able to watch amazing athletes achieve incredible feats on the field.

It still astonishes me when young adults perform at such a high level.

We all know they don't get that good by simply picking up a uniform and showing up on Saturday afternoons. Those kids have prepared for years to play for their school.

We don't see the demanding weight room sessions, the hours of intense coaching on and off the field, and the time they spend alone scouring footage to find the tiniest advantage over their opponent.

We're willing to put in the time to improve at a variety of things in our lives. We'll work overtime at the office to earn a promotion and increase our career opportunities. Gyms are full everyday with folks taking care of their bodies and either getting into or staying in shape. We carve out time to spend with our families so we can improve our role as a spouse or parent.

God deserves the same commitment from us. I cannot imagine if you've made it this far in the book, you haven't discovered at least a few opportunities to improve your relationship and faithfulness with Jesus. Changing your behavior will never be easy.

It takes time and effort, just like all these other areas of life where we desire improvement. Let me assure you the effort is worth it.

Paul tells us, in 1 Timothy 4:7, to train ourselves for godliness. I believe it's a requirement to understand what you're trying to achieve in your life as a steward and what it takes to get there. When we look to improve our spiritual walk with the Lord, it doesn't happen by accident. If you're just swaying as the wind blows in this world, you will continuously be dragged away from your Savior.

You must create new disciplines, maybe even start with a checklist of what needs to be done—not just to say you did it—but to help you start retraining your head, your heart, and your muscle memory.

In Hebrews 12:11 (NIV), we find encouragement. "No discipline seems pleasant at the time, but painful. Later on, it produces a harvest of righteousness and peace for those who have been trained by it."

It's our natural tendency to take our income and use it first for our lifestyle, debt, and taxes, then wonder why there's nothing left to give to church or anyone else. It's perspective every time. The focus is on ourself, then everything else.

When we act like this, we become discontent, enlarge our debt load, and fail to give as Christ instructs us. Instead, be radical. Start giving from your first fruits. Reverse the order of how you spend your money. God commands us in Exodus 23:19 to do just that.

We're bombarded with selfish messages every day—you *need* a newer car and a bigger house. You *need*, you *need*, you *need*. No wonder we give in so often. Our selfish flesh constantly tells us the same thing.

Between our natural tendencies and all the advertisements we soak in daily, of course we're tempted to buy all this stuff.

But our Lord says, "Wait a minute." Remember who graces you with all these gifts in the first place. Remember who takes care of you and provides for you even during the darkest days of your life. Remember who created you and set forth the blueprint for your very existence.

Scripture informs us of all the benefits of applying godly advice to our decisions. (Proverbs 19:8, 20; Colossians 3:23-24) You can't be driven by guilt. You must desire change in your life based on a need to be more generous because of your thankfulness for all God's provided. The challenge of growing your stewardship mindset is to make giving a first thought instead of waiting to see if there's anything left over.

The question now, how do I make sure I have enough to take care of all of my bills and regular expenses if I increase my giving?

To reemphasize, tithe if you're not already doing so. This is a non-negotiable. As a Christian, this is a minimum expectation regardless of your income amount.

Be in constant contact with the Holy Spirit so you can know when He's prompting you to do something extra. Don't miss these opportunities. One example is paying for someone else's groceries at the store. I worked with a couple, and the wife enjoyed doing this. I could tell there was a need to figure out how often she could do this without affecting what they needed for monthly expenses.

So, I offered this idea... what if you set aside a certain amount each month you guys agree on that she can use to help purchase groceries for others? It's a win-win, the giving is still spontaneous as she is prompted, but you've both budgeted for the giving before it occurs.

Both spouses are happy with the plan, and God is pleased because He has cheerful givers obeying and sharing His love.

Use a budgeting plan for your overall giving starting with your tithe. Go ahead and set aside a certain amount of money each month for gifts or giving so it's in the extra savings account waiting for you when the Lord calls.

Trust me, if you're serious about giving more, and you're asking God to show you how to accomplish the task, you will be overwhelmed with the difference you can make for others and yourself.

It can even help strengthen your marriage if you're working the plan together.

———

Apply Today's Truth

- If you want your giving to increase, it won't happen without being purposeful. If you're married, plan a discussion for each of you to list some areas of interest. Having this conversation really helped Christy and me learn new things about each other and form a game plan for increased giving priorities.
- Make sure you have a plan for payday. Your tithe comes out first. Then arrange for other giving, savings, and debt. Plan your lifestyle expenses around the money left over. This will help you decrease your spending on things you don't need.

38

Much Better to Give

In everything I did, I showed you that by this kind of
hard work we must help the weak, remembering the
words the Lord Jesus himself said:
"It is more blessed to give than to receive."
—Acts 20:35 (NIV)

Paul's relationship with the members of the
Ephesian church serves as an example of what true
Christian friendship should be. He helped them learn
how to live as true servants of God during the early
days of the church.

Our Scripture from Acts 20 shows us some of
Paul's final words to his friends in Ephesus as the
Holy Spirit led him away towards Jerusalem. Paul
had worked hard. He left everything on the field
of missions. He considered his life worth nothing.
Everything he did was aimed at spreading the gospel
of Jesus (Acts 20:34).

And then Paul quotes his Savior with a phrase not
recorded anywhere else in the Bible. "It is more blessed
to give than to receive." Just because we don't find
that phrase written elsewhere in the gospels doesn't
mean Jesus didn't say it. John remarks there's no way

a handful of followers could have ever recorded everything Jesus said (John 25:21).

Let's focus on that particular phrase. It's a difficult concept for so many folks to comprehend and actually believe. How is it better to give something than to get something? How can the notion be true? We've all witnessed little kids racing toward the tree on Christmas morning in search of their name on a gift to see what they got. They weren't as concerned with the gifts they were giving to others.

It's a natural tendency of our flesh. We like to get stuff. It's part of our selfish desires we're born with. Any time I give something away, it's guaranteed to diminish how much I can actually possess. I'm subtracting from my personal overall net worth.

Think about how Jesus expects us to live. There's lots of attitudes, reactions, and desires I produce naturally without any help from Jesus. They're all the exact opposite of the attitudes, reactions, and desires He instructs me to have.

We're created and designed in the likeness of God (Genesis 1:27). Therefore, we're expected to think and act like the example He sets for us. God has graciously given to us since the beginning of time.

The most glaring example—He loved us so much that He gave us His only Son (John 3:16). God knew there was no other way for us to live eternally with Him because of our sin. So, He moved His Son from the holy throne and thrust Him into a dark and dying world to rescue you and me.

He didn't just come to visit and teach us. That would have been demeaning enough for a member of the holy family. He came to give His life. The Son of God lowered Himself to live the life of a human man and die the brutal death of a common thief.

God's mercy and grace are some of the other remarkable gifts we receive from God. How tremendous that God knows *exactly* what we need and don't need! The grace of God is *giving* us what we don't deserve—eternity with Him. The mercy of God is *not giving* us what we do deserve—spending all of our days in hell as punishment for our sins.

God's very character is to give. He makes sure to consistently drive home the loving message throughout Scripture.

- Deuteronomy 15:10—Give generously without a grudging heart.
- Proverbs 28:27—Give to the poor.
- Luke 6:38—Give, and it will be given to you.
- 1 Timothy 6:18—Be generous and share.

In Brad Formsma's book *I Like Giving*, the author pieces together story after story to exemplify the importance of following God's script for establishing a lifestyle focused on what we can do for other people. His goal is to remind us how giving needs to be a major part of our lives. It's what we're designed to do. Formsma says, "Joy doesn't come from filling your life with stuff. Joy comes from giving your life away."[25]

God assures us we will not regret believing Him and living out this principle in our lives. Look at the promises He lays out in the verses listed above. If we give generously and with a willing heart, God will bless our work, make sure we lack for nothing, and He will give back to us as we have given to Him and to others.

There's usually a lot of doubt with these verses. How in the world can I receive so much if I'm handing it all away? We continue to look at things in our worldly ways. We think about numbers. We don't think the way God thinks. It's not the way He's teaching us to see things either.

If I give to someone in need because God asks me to, I'm living in the will that God has set forth for my life. I'm living out the purpose I was designed for. If I'm hanging out in the sweet spot of my faith and my obedience of God, look out. My earthly checking account might not increase, but my heavenly account will begin to overflow.

Luke 6:38 (NIV) is one of my favorite promises from God. "Give, and it will be given to you. A good measure, pressed down, shaken together and running over, will be poured into your lap. For the measure you use, it will be measured to you."

If you give unselfishly, God will give unselfishly to you. If you give others an unforgiving heart, selfishness or prideful attitude—guess what?

Whatever measure you use will be given back to you. God has promised I cannot out give Him. Try Him.

You'll be proven wrong every time. Our loving God wants so badly for us to experience His blessings! This verse in Luke 6 deals with the way we interact with others. Do we judge too harshly? Do we not give mercy when we should? Do we keep to ourselves what God wants us to share with others?

How do we want God and others to treat us? The same way we should be giving to others through our attitudes, our knowledge, and our resources.

—◦∿◦—

Apply Today's Truth

- Do you honestly believe Jesus' words about giving? Are you denying God an opportunity to use you as a vessel for His work?
- Pray God will open your eyes to situations and ministries He's preparing you for in your neighborhood or city where He is meeting physical and spiritual needs.

39

The Debt to Love One Another

*Let no debt remain outstanding, except the continuing
debt to love one another, for whoever loves others has
fulfilled the law. The commandments... are summed up
in this one command; "Love your neighbor as yourself."
Love does no harm to a neighbor.
Therefore love is the fulfillment of the law.*
—Romans 13:8-10 (NIV)

These verses highlight one of the basic tenets of
our faith—how we are to first love our Holy
God and then show love for each other. What a simple
concept. How much different would our world be
today if we all simply followed these two rules?

Sin will always wreak havoc on our fallen world,
but so much destruction would be avoided if we were
all working day-by-day to lead lifestyles of faith. The
pride and selfishness reigns out of control destroying
lives and relationships. People commit unspeak-
able acts because they no longer have regard for even
human life.

Go back and review the Ten Commandments.
You can break down the commandments into two
separate groups. We should first love our Father. The

first four commandments spell out those instructions. He speaks of creating idols in your life and honoring His name and His Sabbath.

These commandments are all associated with our relationship with God. If we can't get these in order first, nothing else matters. I can't show the love of God in my earthly relationships if I'm not living my life for Him the way He intended.

The final six commandments collectively address matters of the heart and how we connect with all of God's other children. They deal with sins committed against our neighbor: stealing, killing, desiring and taking their spouses, craving their stuff. Romans 13:8-10 focuses on the crux of those commands. Let love be your only debt. If you love others, you have done all the Law demands.

God's message is simple. Love others the way He loves us. If we spent our days searching for ways to serve other people—a kind gesture, going out of our way to raise someone's spirits, sacrificing a personal luxury to give to someone in need—how much more fulfilled would our lives be? The apostle John confirmed this when he wrote, "Since God so loved us, we also ought to love one another" (1 John 4:12 NIV).

As Christians, we have been granted access to the mind of Christ (1 Corinthians 2:16). Through the Holy Spirit, we are able to tap into the thoughts and intentions of God Almighty. The Spirit helps us, guides us, and lets us know when we venture down a wrong path.

"When [the Holy Spirit] comes, He will prove the world to be in the wrong about sin and righteousness and judgment" (John 16:8 NIV).

Our Savior voluntarily removed Himself from His rightful spot sitting on the throne when He assumed life as a human man for thirty-three years. I am a human man. Odds are, I'm pretty confident I would choose the throne if someone gave me the option between the two.

He spent His days on earth teaching us, healing us, and preparing us for God's message. He didn't have to do any of it, not one bit. There was nothing and no one who forced Jesus to take on all the attributes of a human. He experienced the wonderful feelings of love we feel for our families, but He also dealt with unthinkable betrayal from His friends, unfathomable physical pain during His last days, and the extreme loneliness of His own Father leaving Him in His last moments.

Jesus did it all out of love. He allowed His entire earthly existence to be all about loving us.

Of course, we can never achieve the perfection Jesus displayed on earth. Does it mean we shouldn't try? Remember, that achievement wouldn't qualify us for our heavenly home. However, it would show others the love of their Father, and it would help embolden us with confidence in carrying out our heavenly duties here on earth.

When we consider how we treat other people, we should have gratitude on our minds. We should bend over backwards to show thankfulness for the loving Father who suffered a torturous experience on earth to fulfill His ultimate destiny to win over our souls.

He was entirely human and entirely God at the same time. He physically felt the brunt of those excruciating lashes on His back. He mentally experienced the loneliness of being led through the streets carrying His own cross and then being hanged and killed with that very same slab of wood.

When we need an example of how to give and how to care for those around us, it really is as simple as looking to Jesus. He's the only one who has or ever will live a perfect life on this globe.

We owe Him. We owe Him a debt we can never repay. The only thing He asks of us is to love Him and to love our neighbor, and to experience heaven on earth through the peace that He provides and then to share that unexplainable peace to everyone we meet. Is it really too much for our Savior to ask of us?

—◦◦◦—

Apply Today's Truth

- Are you actively searching for ways to love other people? Is it difficult for you to move out of your comfort zone to affect others in a godly way? Ask God for courage and opportunity.

- When you get upset with someone, do you remember God's command is to still love that person? It's not easy to do. Spend time with God's Word to help you better understand and prepare for times of strife in your relationships.

40

Encouragement for Your Journey

Let us not become weary in doing good,
for at the proper time we will reap a harvest
if we do not give up.
—Galatians 6:9 (NIV)

If you've worked your way through this book, putting in time for additional study and conversation with Christ, there's no doubt, by now, the Holy Spirit has pointed out some aspects of your life that require your attention.

Please keep going. Do not stop here!

This is only the beginning of your journey. Now is the time for daily life-changing application.

You've studied a large amount of Scripture dealing with the topic of developing a stewardship mindset. Hopefully, the information has challenged you to see new ways to grow in your relationship with Christ.

We are considered "on the clock" for God until we take our final breath. We're held accountable for working on our process of sanctification. Like a new home, we lay the foundation and then build it up brick-by-brick with God overseeing the lifetime project.

What now? It's time to apply the principles the Holy Spirit has revealed to you. I pray you've already changed your behavior or started new habits as you've begun seeing things in a different light. Maybe you're already experiencing the blessings we've discussed from discovering ways to be more generous with your money, your spiritual gifts, and your time. You will find more of the joy God promises in your life if you're following His commands.

A word of warning - it doesn't get easier from here. The outside world will try to confuse you with its attraction of self-gratification and sinful practices. Satan will lie and deceive you, attempting to pull you back to a mindset built on pleasing yourself while casting others aside.

Be encouraged by the words spoken by Paul in Galatians 6:9 (NIV). "Let us not become weary in doing good, for at the proper time we will reap a harvest if we do not give up."

Remember the uneasiness and discomfort of doing things your way. You didn't save enough. Your debt load continued to grow larger. You spent way too much money on a lifestyle that didn't honor God. You've now learned the remedy to these situations. God has a plan full of biblical principles waiting for you to adopt so you can begin finding contentment and peace in your everyday life. Now it's simply time to get to work.

In 1 Chronicles 28:20 (NIV), we find an aging King David advising his son Solomon on the daunting task of building the temple in the way God has instructed. The plans are intricate, and it's a mountain of a task for the new king to oversee. David tells his son, "Be strong and courageous, and do the work. Do not be afraid or discouraged, for the Lord God, my God, is with you. He will not fail you or forsake you until all the work for the service of the temple of the Lord is finished."

Do the work.

Simply do the work. God is with you and will watch after you.

It's time to formulate your plan. Where do you start? Where do you feel the Holy Spirit convicting you in your stewardship life? Don't try to take on dozens of principles and apply them to your daily living all at once. That's way too much and sets you up for nearly certain failure.

Instead, consider the top two or three areas that you and the Spirit agree are ones that need some work. Prioritize what you'd like to achieve and then set very particular goals to see them through.

Remember what we discussed earlier about paying down debt. The same rules apply here. You must be specific in what you plan to do and have a way to measure the results. You might've seen the easy way to remember the principles of goal setting. You can use the acronym SMART.

Specific
Measurable
Attainable
Relevant
Timely

State the precise goal and how you will keep track of your progress. Make sure it's something achievable and that it makes sense in your situation.

For instance, you and your spouse plan to purchase a new home in the next few years, and you'd like to save enough cash for the 20% down payment to avoid the additional mortgage insurance. If the purchase price is $150,000, you'll be required to save $30,000. That's a specific goal.

You've looked at your finances and found a couple of places to cut costs in your monthly budget. By doing so, you could save $500 per month toward the new home purchase.

At that rate, you could save $6,000 per year. In five years, you'll have enough for the down payment. Your goal is specific, measurable, attainable, relevant, and timely.

Don't be afraid to challenge yourself, but never set a goal you know you just can't achieve. Doing so simply sets you up for heartbreak and devastation.

My mission is to keep you motivated and moving forward. You can do this! Remember, it's not just about placing checkmarks on the checklist. God desires to share His wisdom and His excitement for giving with you.

He's rooting for you and cheering you on. We find examples of an encouraging Father throughout Scripture.

When we're working on task for Him, we know we have a purpose in our activity. "Therefore, my dear brothers, stand firm. Let nothing move you. Always give yourselves fully to the work of the Lord, because you know that your labor in the Lord is not in vain." (1 Corinthians 15:58 NIV)

"For God did not give us a spirit of timidity, but a spirit of power, of love, and of self-discipline." (2 Timothy 1:7 NIV)

Doing the right thing isn't easy. If it was, we wouldn't have to try so hard to do it. It's worth the struggles, the pain, and the effort of pleasing our Savior and showing Him how much we love Him and appreciate Him. Your work will not be in vain. He provides us with a powerful spirit of self-discipline.

Get to work. Change the path you're on by trusting God and His principles of stewardship. Make wise financial decisions - spend less, save more, eliminate debt, and multiply your giving in every conceivable way.

I can't wait for you to discover the ultimate peace, joy, and contentment God has to offer when you're pursuing spiritual wealth.

Apply Today's Truth

- I challenge you to design a game plan. Don't just put this book down and be done with learning about stewardship. List at least a couple of areas in your life needing attention now. Should you work more on handling finances, discovering your spiritual gifts, or contributing more of your time to work for God's kingdom?

- How can you enhance your education on the topic of stewardship? Can you speak with a class administrator or pastor in your church about providing more education for your church family? How can you help friends and family understand the topic and their responsibilities more clearly?

Notes

Notes

Stewardship Resources

Additional ways to study and apply stewardship lessons:

Master Your Money: A Step-By-Step Plan for Experiencing Financial Contentment by Ron Blue with Michael Blue—personal study book based on biblical principles to help with money management and financial planning

God Owns It All: Finding Contentment and Confidence in Your Finances by Ron Blue with Michael Blue—six-week study appropriate for personal use or with small study group

The Financial Stewardship Bible (Contemporary English Version) by the American Bible Society—highlights verses relative to stewardship and money management

Crown MoneyLife Indicator—https://mli2.crown.org—questionnaire to help assess current personal thoughts and actions towards stewardship

Crown Ministries—Estimate Budget Worksheet—https://www.crown.org/wp-content/uploads/ 2018/ 02/EstimatedBudgetW.pdf

Bibliography

1. Billy Graham Evangelistic Association, "5 Things the Bible Says About Work," August 27, 2018, https://billygraham.org/story/5-things-the-bible-says-about-work/.

2. https://www.forbes.com/sites/kevinkruse/2013/04/09/what-is-leadership/?sh=4976bd5f5b90

3. Kingdom Advisors, Inc. (2018). *Certified Kingdom Advisor Education Program*. U.S.A.

4. Barna, Dr. George, 2020, "Inaugural CRC Study: Dangerously Low Percentage of Americans Hold Biblical Worldview," *American Worldview Inventory 2020*. Article published by Arizona Christian University News, March 24, 2020. https://www.arizonachristian. edu/blog/2020/03/24/inaugural-crc-study-danger-ously-low-percentage-of-americans-hold-bibli-cal-worldview/.

5. Lennick, Doug, CFP® with Kathleen Jordan, Ph.D. (2010). *Financial Intelligence: How to Make Smart, Values-Based Decisions with Your Money and Your Life*. FPA Press, Denver, CO.

6. Collins, Brandon; Warren, Michael; Ryan, Travis. (2015) "Until My Voice is Gone" [Recorded by Travis Ryan]. *On You Hold It All (Live)*. Lyrics obtained from "Until My Voice is Gone" (Lyric Video) on YouTube.

7. Kingdom Advisors, Inc. (2018). *Certified Kingdom Advisor Education Program.* U.S.A.

8. Calonia, Jennifer. "Average American Debt." Bankrate, March 23, 2020. https://www.bankrate.com/finance/debt/average-american-debt/.

9. Leonhardt, Megan. "Here's How Much Americans Have at Every Age." CNBC, August 20, 2018. https://www.cnbc.com/2018/08/20/how-much-debt-americans-have-at-every-age.html.

10. Schmall, Tyler. "Americans Spend Half Their Lives in Front of Screens." New York Post, August 13, 2018. https://nypost.com/2018/08/13/americans-spend-half-their-lives-in-front-of-screens/.

11. Bentley, Chuck. "His, Hers or Ours?" Focus on the Family, January 1, 2015. https://www.focusonthefamily.com/marriage/his-hers-or-ours/.

12. Zhen, Simon. "Study: 1 in 5 Americans Spend More Time Planning Vacations vs. Managing Their Money." My Banktracker, July 30, 2019. https://www.mybanktracker.com/open-data/surveys/survey-time-planning-vacations-managing-money-301436

13. Blue, Ron. "Live, Give, Owe, Grow Numbers Tool". Kingdom Advisors, August 2015. https://kingdomadvisors.com/resources/live-give-owe-grow-excel-tool-1

14. American Bible Society (1995). *The Financial Stewardship Bible (Contemporary English Version)*. American Bible Society, New York.

15. Moody, DL (1895). *Pleasure and Profit in Bible Study*. The Bible Institute Colportage Association, Minneapolis, MN.

16. Pryor, Austin. "7 Key Principles for Christian Living." Sound Mind Investing, 2018. https://www.crown.org/wp-content/uploads/2018/08/7-Key-Principles-for-Christian-Investing.pdf

17. "U.S. Texting Statistics". The Local Project, last accessed September 10, 2020. https://www.local-project.net/docs/texting-stats/.

18. Kobliner, Beth. "Money Habits Are Set By Age 7. Teach Your Kids the Value of a Dollar Now." PBS, April 5, 2018. https://www.pbs. org/newshour/economy/making-sense/money-habits-are-set-by-age-7-teach-your-kids-the-value-of-a-dollar-now.

19. Kingdom Advisors, Inc. (2018). *Certified Kingdom Advisor Education Program*. U.S.A.

20. Jeremiah, David. "What Kind of Rewards Will Believers Receive in Heaven?" David Jeremiah Blog, last accessed September 10, 2020. https://davidjeremiah.blog/what-kind-of-rewards-will-believers-receive-in-heaven/.

21. Robertson, Pat. Interview with Dr. Robert Jeffress. *The 700 Club.* Christian Broadcasting Network (CBN), unknown date of interview, last accessed September 10, 2020. https://www1.cbn.com/prepare-yourself-heaven.

22. Graham, Billy. "Are You Robbing God?" Decision: The Evangelical Voice for Today, November 1, 2018. https://decisionmagazine.com/ are-you-robbing-god/.

23. Kimbro, Dennis and Napoleon Hill (2011). *Think and Grow Rich: A Black Choice: A Guide to Success for Black Americans.* The Random House Publishing Group, New York.

24. Graham, Billy. "Relying on Grace - Daily Devotion". Billy Graham Evangelistic Association, last accessed September 10, 2020. https://billygraham.org/devotion/relying-on-grace/.

25. Formsma, Brad (2014). *I Like Giving: The Transforming Power of a Generous Life.* WaterBrook Press, Colorado Springs, CO.

About the Author

Marcus Hall is an author and Christian financial advisor, helping families create and develop values based planning, investment, and giving strategies. His goal is to help people understand the biblical principles of stewardship, how to apply them to real life, and fulfill

God's purpose for their existence. He's gained valuable knowledge on the subject by obtaining the Certified Kingdom Advisor® designation and desires to help people integrate their Christian values into their financial decision making.

Marcus spent the early part of his career as a broadcast journalist and was awarded multiple Alabama Associated Press Awards for his anchoring, reporting, and videography of local high school and college sports events. His passion was finding that something special about local athletes, both kids and adults, and sharing their stories with his audience. He now uses those same skills honed in the broadcast industry to teach others on the principles of stewardship.

To request Marcus for a media interview or speaking engagement, please email info@stewardship-mindset.com.

To learn more about Marcus, visit his website at www.stewardshipmindset.com.

9 781956 267143